God's Way
of Holiness

Horatius Bonar

Christian Heritage

Christian Focus Publications publishes biblically-accurate books for adults and children. The books in the adult range are published in three imprints.

Christian Heritage contains classic writings from the past.

Christian Focus contains popular works including biographies, commentaries, doctrine, and Christian living.

Mentor focuses on books written at a level suitable for Bible College and seminary students, pastors, and others; the imprint includes commentaries, doctrinal studies, examination of current issues, and church history.

For a free catalogue of all our titles, please write to
Christian Focus Publications,
Geanies House, Fearn,
Ross-shire, IV20 1TW, Great Britain

For details of our titles visit us on our web site
http://www.christianfocus.com

ISBN 1 85792 503 3

© Christian Focus Publications
Published in 1999
by
Christian Focus Publications
Geanies House, Fearn,
Ross-shire, IV20 1TW, Great Britain

Cover design by Owen Daily

Contents

PREFACE

The way of peace and the way of holiness lie side by side; or rather, they are one. That which bestows the peace imparts the holiness; and he who takes the one of these takes the other also. The Spirit of peace is the Spirit of holiness. The God of peace is the God of holiness.

If, at any time, these paths seem to go asunder, there must be something wrong; wrong in the teaching that makes them seem to part company, or wrong in the state of the man in whose life they have done so.

They start together; or at least so nearly together that no eye, save the divine, can mark a difference. Yet, properly speaking, the peace goes before the holiness, and is its parent. This is what divines call priority in nature, though not in time; which means substantially this, that the difference in such almost identical beginnings, is too small in point of time, to be perceived by us; yet is it not on that account the less distinct and real. The two are not independent. There is fellowship between them, vital fellowship; each being the helpmeet of the other. The fellowship is not of mere coincidence, as in the case of strangers who happen to meet on the same path; nor of arbitrary appointment, as in the case of two parallel roads; but of mutual help and sympathy; like the fellowship of head and heart, or of two members of one body; the peace being indispensable to the production or causation of the holiness, and the holiness indispensable to the maintaining and deepening of the peace.

He who affirms that he has peace, while living in sin,

is 'a liar, and the truth is not in him.' He who thinks that he has holiness, though he has no peace, ought to question whether he understands aright what the Bible means by either the one or the other; for as the essence of holiness is the soul's right state toward God, it does not seem possible that a man can be holy, so long as there is no conscious reconciliation between God and him. A spurious holiness there may be, founded upon a spurious peace, or upon no peace at all; but true holiness must start from a true and authentic peace.

Kelso, July 1864

CHAPTER 1

THE NEW LIFE

And I will give them one heart, and I will put a new spirit within you; and I will take the stony heart out of their flesh, and will give them an heart of flesh (Ezek. 11:19).

A new heart also will I give you, and a new spirit will I put within you; and I will take away the stony heart out of your flesh, and I will give you an heart of flesh (Ezek. 36:26).

Therefore we are buried with him by baptism into death; that like as Christ was raised up from the dead by the glory of the Father, even so we also should walk in newness of life (Rom. 6:4).

Therefore if any man be in Christ he is a new creature: old things are passed away; behold all things are become new (2 Cor. 5:17).

For in Christ Jesus neither circumcision availeth any thing, nor uncircumcision, but a new creature (Gal. 6:15).

And that ye put on the new man, which after God is created in righteousness and true holiness (Eph. 4:24).

And have put on the new man, which is renewed in knowledge after the image of him that created him (Col. 3:10).

As newborn babes, desire the sincere milk of the word, that ye may grow thereby (1 Pet. 2:2).

Whereby are given unto us exceeding great and precious promises; that by these ye might be partakers of the divine nature, having escaped the corruption that is in the world through lust (2 Pet. 1:4).

It is to a new life that God is calling us; not to some new steps in life, some new habits or ways or motives or prospects, but to *a new life*.

For the production of this new life the eternal Son of God took flesh, died, was buried, and rose again.

It is not life producing life, a lower life rising into a higher, but life rooting itself in its opposite, life *wrought out of death*, by the death of 'the Prince of life'. Of the new creations, as of the old, he is the author.

For the working out of this the Holy Spirit came down in power, entering men's souls and dwelling there, that out of the old he might bring forth the new.

That which God calls *new* must be so indeed. For the Bible means what it says; as being, of all books, not only the most true in thought, but the most accurate in speech. Great then and authentic must be that 'new thing in the earth' which God 'creates;' to which he calls us; and which he brings about by such stupendous means and at such a cost. Most hateful also must that old life of ours be to him, when in order to abolish it, he delivers up his Son; and most dear must we be in his sight when in order to rescue us from the old life, and make us partakers of the new, he brings forth all the divine resources of love and power and wisdom, to meet the exigencies of a case which would otherwise have been wholly desperate.

The man from whom the old life has gone out, and into whom the new life has come, is still the same individual. The same being that was once 'under law' is now 'under grace'. His features and limbs are still the same; his intellect, imagination, capacities and responsibilities are still the same. But yet old things have passed away; all things have become new. The old man is slain, the new

man lives. It is not merely the old life retouched and made
more comely, defects struck out, roughnesses smoothed
down, graces stuck on here and there. It is not a broken
column repaired, a soiled picture cleaned, a defaced
inscription filled up, an unswept temple white-washed. It
is more than all this, else God would not call it a *new
creation*, nor would the Lord have affirmed with such
awful explicitness, as he does, in his conference with
Nicodemus, the divine law of exclusion from and entrance
into the kingdom of God (John 3:3). Yet how few in our
day believe that 'that which is born of the flesh is flesh,
and that which is born of the Spirit is Spirit' (John 3:6).

Hear how God speaks! He calls us '*new*-born babes'
(1 Pet. 2:2); '*new* creatures' (Gal. 6: 15); a '*new* lump'
(1 Cor. 5:7); a '*new* man' (Eph. 2:15); doers of 'a *new*
commandment' (1 John 2:8); heirs of 'a *new* name' and a
'*new* city' (Rev. 2:17; 3:12); expectants of '*new* heavens
and a *new* earth' (2 Pet. 3:13). This *new* being, having
begun in a *new* birth, unfolds itself in '*newness* of spirit'
(Rom. 7:6); according to a '*new* covenant' (Heb. 8:8);
walks along a '*new* and living way' (Heb. 10:20); and ends
in the '*new* song' and the '*new* Jerusalem' (Rev. 5:9; 21:2).

So that it is no outer thing, made up of showy moralities
and benevolences; or picturesque rites and a graceful
routine of devotion; or sentimentalisms bright or sombre;
or religious utterances on fit occasions, as to the grandeur
of antiquity, or sacramental grace, or the greatness of
creaturehood, or the nobleness of humanity, or the
universal fatherhood of God. It is something deeper, and
truer, and more genial, than that which is called deep, and
true, and genial in modern religious philosophy. Its
affinities are with the things above; its sympathies are

divine; it sides with God in everything; it has nothing, beyond a few expressions, in common with the superficialities and falsehoods which, under the name of religion, are current among multitudes who call Christ Lord and master.

A Christian is one who has been 'crucified with Christ,' who has died with him, been buried with him, risen with him, ascended with him, and is seated 'in heavenly places' with him (Rom. 6:3-8; Gal. 2:20; Eph. 2:5,6; Col. 3:1-3). As such he 'reckons himself dead unto sin, but alive unto God' (Rom. 6:11). As such he does not yield his members instruments of unrighteousness unto sin; but he 'yields himself unto God as alive from the dead, and his members as instruments of righteousness unto God'. As such he 'seeks the things which are above,' and sets his affection on things above, 'mortifying his members which are upon the earth, fornication, uncleanness, inordinate affection, evil concupiscence and covetousness, which is idolatry' (Col. 3:5).

This newness is comprehensive, both in its exclusion of the evil and its inclusion of the good. It is summed up by the apostle in two things, 'righteousness and holiness'; 'put off,' says he, '*the old man,* who is corrupt, according to the deceitful lusts, and be *renewed* in the spirit of your mind; put on the *new man,* which, after God, is created in righteousness and true holiness' (Eph. 4:22-24, literally 'righteousness and holiness of the truth,' that is, resting on or springing out of *the truth*). The new man then is meant to be *righteous* and *holy,* inwardly and outwardly, before God and man, as respects law and gospel, and this *through the truth.* For as that which is false ('the lie,' verse 25) can only produce unrighteousness and unholiness; so the truth produces righteousness and holiness, through the power of the Holy Ghost. Error injures, truth heals; error is the root of sin, truth of purity and perfection.

It is then to a new standing or state, a new moral character, a new life, a new joy, a new work, a new hope, that we are called. And he who thinks that religion comprises anything less than this knows nothing yet as he ought to know. To that which *man* calls 'piety,' less may suffice; but to no religion which does not in some degree embrace these, can the divine recognition be accorded.

These are weighty words of the apostle, 'we are *his workmanship*.[1] Of him, and through him, and to him, are all things pertaining to us. Chosen, called, quickened, washed, sanctified and justified by God himself, we are, in no sense, our own deliverers. The quarry out of which the marble comes is his; the marble itself is his; the digging and hewing and polishing are his; he is the sculptor and we the statue.

'We are his workmanship,' says the apostle. But this is not all. We are, he adds, 'created in Christ Jesus unto good works, which God hath before ordained that we should walk in them.' The plan, the selection of the materials, the model, the workman, the workmanship, are all divine; and though it does not yet appear what we shall be, we know that we shall be 'like him', his image reproduced in us, himself represented by us; for we are 'renewed after the image of him that created us' (Col. 3:10).

It is not, however, dead, cold marble that is to be

---

1. Eph. 2:10. See also Deut. 32:6; Pss. 103:3; 138:8; Isa. 43:21; 40:21; Rom. 9:21; Heb. 13:21; Jas. 1:18. Our object in citing these passages is to show how entirely our new character is a *divine* creation, the result of a *divine* purpose, in all its parts.

wrought upon. That is simple work; requiring just a given amount of skill. But the remoulding of the soul is unspeakably more difficult, and requires far more complex appliances. The influences at work in opposing, internal and external, spiritual, legal, physical, are many; and equally numerous must be the influences brought into play to meet all these, and carry out the design. The work is not mechanical, but moral and spiritual (physical in a sense, as dealing with the *nature* of things, but, more truly, moral and spiritual); and omnipotence is not mere unlimited physical power, operating, as upon inanimate matter, by mere intensity of volition; but power which, with unlimited resources at command, exhibits its greatness by regulating its forthgoings according to moral circumstances, producing its greatest results by indirect moral influences, developing itself in conformity with law and sovereignty and holy love on the one hand, and on the other with human guilt and creature responsibility and free volition. The complexities thus introduced are infinite, and the 'variable quantities,' if one may so speak, are so peculiar and so innumerable, that we can find no formula to help us in the solution of the problem; we get bewildered in speculating on the processes by which omnipotence deals with moral beings, either in their sinfulness or their holiness.

And here let us notice the *duality* or twofoldness of divine truth; the overlooking of which has occasioned much fruitless controversy and originated many falsehoods. Truth is, indeed, not *two-sided,* but *many-sided*, like a well-cut crystal. In a more general sense, however, it is truly *double*; with a heavenly and an earthly, a divine and a human side or aspect. It is at the line where these two meet that the greatest nicety of adjustment is required; and hence it is here that divergent theologies have come specially into conflict. The heavenward and the earthward aspect of truth must be carefully distinguished; the one fitting into the other; the one the counterpart of the other. God is absolute Sovereign – this is the one side; man has volition of his own, and is not a machine or a stone – that is the other. God chooses and draws according to the good pleasure of his will; yet he hinders no man from coming or from willing. God is the giver of faith, yet faith cometh by hearing, and hearing by the word of God (Rom. 10:17).[2] God worketh in us both to will and to do; yet he commands us to work out our salvation with fear and trembling. It is God that sanctifies us, yet it is through 'the truth' that we are sanctified (John 17:17). It is God that purifies (Tit. 2:14); yet it is by faith that our hearts are purified (Acts 15:9). It is God that fills us with joy and peace; and yet this is 'in believing.' It is God that renews; yet we read, 'make you a new heart' (Ezek. 18:31). The movements of man's faculties are not superseded by God, but assumed and regulated; the intellect is not overborne and deforced, but set free to work

---

2. Hence the difficulty of believing is not from the absence of proper faculties, but from the derangement of these; and conversion is God's restoration of these to their original nature. *Faith* is not a foreign gem imported into the soul, distinct from all our original powers, it is simply *the man believing,* in consequence of his soul being set right by the Holy Spirit; but he believes and disbelieves in the same way as before. It is not the intellect, or the mind, or the affections, that believe, it is *the man,* the whole man; the same whole man that formerly disbelieved. Very absurd and unphilosophical (not to say unscriptural) have been the questions raised as to the *seat* of faith, whether it is in the intellect, or the will, or the heart. Faith is *the man believing,* just as love is *the man loving.* In Romans 10:9, the apostle is not contrasting

its true work truly.[3] The 'heavenly things' and 'earthly things' are distinct, yet not separate; always to be viewed in connection with each other, yet not confused; for confusion here works mysticism, superstition and false doctrine. 'There are *celestial* bodies, and bodies *terrestrial;* but the glory of the *celestial* is one, and the glory of the *terrestrial* is another' (1 Cor. 15:40). In every Bible truth there are two elements, the divine and the human; but the divine element is one thing, the human another. The theology that embodies most truth is that which knows how to recognise both of these, without confusion, yet without isolation or antagonism, and which refuses to merge either the divine in the human or the human in the divine.[4]

---

the *heart* with the *mind,* but with the *mouth;* in other words, the inner with the outer man.

3. The more thoroughly we can study the Word of God, the better; and all critical helps are to be welcomed. Genuine scholarship, consecrated to the elucidation of the Word, is an accomplishment of no common price. Everything that brings our souls into full contact with the Word, in its fullness and variety, so as to steep them in it, is to be greatly prized, as fitted to make us holier, more fruitful, and more spiritual men.

4. We hear much of the divine and the human element in Scripture; nor is the expression amiss; yet might we not rather say that the Bible is all human and yet all divine. It is PERFECT *according to what God meant it to be,* though *we* may note what *we* call 'imperfections' in it. The mountains of earth, in their ruggedness, are perfect in their way, though they have not the artificial perfection of the statue or the temple. God has chosen that his book and his world should resemble each other in that kind of perfection, a perfection which man appreciates in the landscape, but depreciates in the Bible.

Hence the necessity for confining ourselves to the Word, and the danger of introducing human metaphysics into questions connected with the spiritual change wrought on us. It is God that worketh; it is we who are wrought upon; and everything needful to be known in connection with this work is revealed in the divine record. We give this thought some prominence, because of the tendency with many to magnify humanity, and to undervalue the greatness of that change, which begins the Christian course and character. No elevation of natural taste, no infusion of religious or benevolent earnestness, no cultivation of the intellect, can fill up the description given us in the Word of one 'who fears God' and is the 'called according to his purpose'; 'begotten again to a lively hope by the resurrection of Jesus Christ from the dead.' And we urge this the more decidedly, because, as is the beginning, so will be the middle and the end. A false idea, or a diverging step at the outset, may lead to a false religion throughout life, to an imperfect and superficial goodness, as one incorrect figure or sign in an equation falsifies both process and result. If the dislocated joint is not properly set, it will never work comfortably; and if the wound is merely skinned over, the disease may be taking its own way underneath; all the more fatally because it is supposed to be removed.

How the Holy Spirit operates in producing the *newness* of which we have spoken, we know not; yet we know that he does not destroy or reverse man's faculties; he renovates them all, so that they fulfil the true ends for which they were given. As he does not make the hand the foot, nor the eye the ear, so he does not make the heart the intellect, nor the will the judgement. Each faculty remains the same in end and use as before, only purified and set properly to work. Nor does the Holy Spirit supersede the use of our faculties by his indwelling. Rather does this indwelling make these more serviceable, more energetic, each one doing his proper work and fulfilling his proper office; while the whole man, body, soul, and spirit, is, instead of being brought under mechanical constraint, made more truly free; never more fully *himself,* than when filled with the Holy Spirit. For the result of the indwelling of the 'free Spirit' is liberty; not bondage, or the production of an artificial character.

Thus, then, though no violence is done to our being, in regeneration, omnipotence is at work at every point. Our new being is not the result of a mechanical process, yet it is the produce of divine power. God claims it as a 'creation,' and as his own handiwork. 'He that hath *wrought us* for the selfsame thing is God' (2 Cor. 5:5); where the word implies the thorough elaboration of some difficult piece of work. 'It is God which worketh in us both to will and to do of his good pleasure' (Phil. 2:13); where the expressions indicate an operation which influences our 'willing' as well as our 'doing;' and this on account of his 'well-pleasedness' (as the word is); his 'well-pleasedness' with Christ (Matt. 3:17) and with his own eternal design. 'God's tillage' (or husbandry, 1 Cor. 3:9) is his name for us when speaking as a husbandman; 'God's building' (or fabric), his name when speaking as an architect. It is to *the image of his Son* that he has 'predestinated us to be conformed, that he might be the first-born among many brethren' (Rom. 8:29); having 'chosen us in him before the foundation of the world, that we should be holy and without blame before him in love' (Eph. 1:4).

It is, then, 'to *holiness*' that God is calling us (1 Thess. 4:7); that we should have our 'fruit unto *holiness*' (Rom. 6:22), that our hearts should be 'stablished unblameable in *holiness*' (1 Thess. 3:13); that we should abound in 'all *holy* conversation and godliness' (2 Pet. 3:11); that we should be 'a *holy* priesthood' (1 Pet. 2:5); '*holy* in all manner of conversation' (1 Pet. 1:15); 'called with a *holy* calling' (2 Tim. 1:9); '*holy* and without blame before him in love' (Eph. 1:4), presenting not our souls alone but our 'bodies as (not only a living but) a *holy* sacrifice to God' (Rom. 12:1), nay, remembering that these bodies are not merely 'a sacrifice,' but 'a *temple* of the Holy Ghost' (1 Cor. 6:19).

Holiness is likeness to God; to him who is the Holy One of Israel; to him whom they laud in heaven, as 'Holy, holy, holy' (Rev. 4:8). It is likeness to Christ; to 'that holy thing' which was born of the Virgin; to him who was 'holy, harmless, undefiled, separate from sinners' (Heb. 7:26). It is not only disjunction from evil, and from an evil world; but it is separation unto God and his service. It is priestly separation, for priestly service. It is distinctiveness such as that which marked the tabernacle and all its vessels; separation from every common use; separation by blood, 'the blood of the everlasting covenant;' this blood (or that which it signifies, death) being interposed between us and all common things, so that we are dead to sin, but alive unto God, alive to righteousness, having died and risen in him whose blood has made us what we are, *saints*, holy ones.

This holiness or consecration extends to every part of our persons; fills up our being, spreads over our life, influences everything we are, or do, or think or speak, or plan, small or great, outward or inward, negative or positive, our living, our hating, our sorrowing, our rejoicing, our recreations, our business, our friendships, our relationships, our silence, our speech, our reading, our writing, our going out and our coming in; our whole man in every moment of spirit, soul, and body. In the house, the sanctuary, the chamber, the market, the shop, the desk, the highway, it must be seen that ours is a *consecrated life*.

In one aspect, sanctification is an *act*, a thing done at once, like justification. The moment the blood touches us, that is, as soon as we believe God's testimony to the blood, we are 'clean' (John 15:3), 'sanctified,' set apart for God (See Appendix, Note 1). It is in this ceremonial or priestly sense that the word is used in the Epistle to the Hebrews; for as that to the Romans takes us into the *forum* and deals with our *legal* standing, so that to the Hebrews takes us into the *temple* and deals with our *priestly* standing. As the vessels of the sanctuary were *at once* separated to God and his service, the moment the blood touched them, so are we. This did not imply that these vessels required no daily ablution afterwards; so neither does our consecration intimate that we need no daily sanctifying, no inward process for getting rid of sin. The initiatory consecration through the blood is one thing, and the continual sanctifying by the power of the Holy Ghost is another. The former is the first step, the introduction to the latter; nay, absolutely indispensable to any progress in the latter; yet it does not supersede it, but makes it rather a greater necessity. To this very end are we consecrated by the blood, that we may be *purified inwardly* by the Holy Ghost; and he who would make the completeness of the former act a substitute for the latter process, or a reason for neglecting it, has yet

to learn what consecration means, what is the import of
the blood which consecrates, and for what end we were
chosen in Christ and called by his grace (Eph. 1:5-7).

The thing which *man* calls sin may be easily obliterated
or toned down into goodness. It deserved no expulsion
from Paradise, no deluge, no Sodom-fire; it is a thing which
the flames of Sinai greatly exaggerate, and of which
Israel's history presents an exceptional picture. It is one
of the mishaps of humanity, the enormity of which has
been quite misreckoned by theologians, and the history of
which, in Scripture, must be read with abatements and
due allowances for oriental colouring! It is not a thing for
the judge, but for the physician; not a thing for
condemnation, but for pity. It deserves no hell, no divine
wrath, no legal sentence; it needs no atonement, no blood,
no cross, no substitution of life for life; mere incarnation
as the expressions of divine love to the unfortunate, and
the intimation to the universe of God's all-comprehending
fatherhood (See Appendix, Note 2), and of Adamhood's
union with God, will be sufficient. But that which God
calls sin is something infinitely terrible, far beyond our
ideas of misfortune and disease, something to which even
Sodom and Sinai gave but faint expression. It is something
which the law curses and the judge condemns; something
which needs a righteous pardon, a divine Saviour, and an
almighty Spirit; something which can destroy a soul and
ruin a world, which can, from one single drop, overflow
earth for six thousand years, and fill hell eternally. It is
that of whose hatefulness the blood and smoke and fire of
the altar speak; which is 'exceeding sinful'; whose wages
is death, the first and second death, and of whose
balefulness the everlasting darkness is the witness.

He who would know holiness must understand sin; and he who would see sin as God sees it, and think of it as God does, must look at the cross and grave of the Son of God, must know the meaning of Gethsemane and Golgotha.[5]

The tendency of the present day is to underestimate *sin* and to misunderstand its nature. From the cross of Christ men strike out the very elements which intimate the divine opinion of its evil; and that accursed tree is not recognised as a condemnation of sin, but simply as an exhibition of self-surrender in a noble sufferer. It is admitted to be an evil, greater or less according to circumstances; a hereditary poison, which time and earnestness will work out of the constitution; an unruly but inevitable appetite, which is to be corrected gradually by moral discipline and wholesome intellectual diet, rendered medicinal by a moderate infusion of the 'religious element'; a sickening pain, sometimes in the conscience, sometimes in the heart, which is to be soothed by the dreamy mysticism, which, acting like spiritual chloroform, dulls the uneasiness without touching its seat; this is all! Why a loving God

---

5. Am I bound to think of sin as God thinks? Most certainly. Have I no liberty of thinking otherwise? None. You may do so, if you choose to venture, but the consequences are fearful, for error is sin. We are not bound to think as *man* thinks. In this respect we have entire liberty; not tradition, but free thought may be our formula here. But we are bound to think as *God* thinks, not in one thing but in every thing. Woe be to him that presumes to differ from God; *or* reckons it a light matter to be of one mind with him; or tries to prove that the Bible is inaccurate or unintelligible, or but half-inspired, in order to release himself from the responsibility of receiving the whole truth of God, and afford him licence to believe or disbelieve at pleasure, freed from the trammels of a fixed revelation.

should, for so slight and curable an evil, have given over
our world for six thousand years to such sorrow, pain,
tears, weariness, disease and death, as have overflowed it
with so terrible a deluge, is a question which such a theory
of evil leaves unanswered. Yet such are the representations
of sin with which we find a large amount of the literature
and the religion of our day penetrated. Humanity is
struggling upward, nobly self-reliant! The race is elevating
itself (for the Darwinian theory has found its way into
religion); and Christianity is a useful help in this process
of self-regeneration, this development of individual
constitutions, by which perfection is to be reached at last
and the kingdom won! Thus does many a prophet speak
peace when there is none; bent on 'healing the hurt' by
the denial of its deadliness. Of what avail this calling evil
good and good evil, will be in the great day of reckoning,
a coming hour will show.

'Awake to righteousness and sin not,' is God's message
to us (1 Cor. 15:34). 'Be ye holy, for I am holy' (1 Pet.
1:15,16). 'Present your bodies a living sacrifice, holy,
acceptable unto God' (Rom. 12:1). 'Purge out the old
leaven, that ye may be a new lump' (1 Cor. 5:7). 'Let every
one that nameth the name of Christ depart from iniquity'
(2 Tim. 2:19). 'Deny ungodliness and worldly lusts, live
soberly, righteously, and godly in this present world' (Tit.
2:12). 'Be diligent that ye may be found of him in peace,
without spot and blameless' (2 Pet. 3:14). 'Let your
conversation be as it becometh the gospel of Christ' (Phil.
1:27). 'Have no fellowship with the unfruitful works of
darkness, but rather reprove them' (Eph. 5:11). 'Put ye on
the Lord Jesus Christ, and make not provision for the flesh,
to fulfil the lusts thereof' (Rom. 13:14). 'I beseech you as

strangers and pilgrims, abstain from fleshly lusts, which war against the soul' (1 Pet. 2:11).

From sin, then, in every sense and aspect, God is calling us. As exceeding sinful, the abominable thing which he hates and will avenge, he warns us against it. He speaks to us as 'shapen in iniquity and conceived in sin', carrying evil about with us, nay, filled with it and steeped in it; not merely as diseased and requiring medicine, or unfortunate and requiring pity, but as guilty, under law, under sentence, dead in trespasses and sins, with inevitable judgement before us. He neither palliates nor aggravates our case, but calmly tells us the worst; showing us what we are, before calling us to be what he has purposed to make us. From all unholiness and unrighteousness, from all corruption, from all crooked ways, from all disobedience, from all filthiness of the flesh and spirit, he is calling us, in Christ Jesus his Son.

CHAPTER 2

CHRIST FOR US, THE SPIRIT IN US

He that believeth on me, as the scripture hath said, out of his belly shall flow rivers of living water. But this spake he of the Spirit, which they that believe on him should receive: for the Holy Ghost was not yet given; because that Jesus was not yet glorified (John 7:38, 39).

Therefore being justified by faith, we have peace with God through our Lord Jesus Christ: By whom also we have access by faith into this grace wherein we stand, and rejoice in hope of the glory of God. And not only so, but we glory in tribulations also: knowing that tribulation worketh patience; and patience, experience; and experience, hope; and hope maketh not ashamed; because the love of God is shed abroad in our hearts by the Holy Spirit, which is given unto us (Rom. 5:1-5).

And such were some of you: but ye are washed, but ye are sanctified, but ye are justified in the name of the Lord Jesus, and by the Spirit of our God (1 Cor. 6:11).

What! know ye not that your body is the temple of the Holy Ghost which is in you, which ye have of God, and ye are not your own? (1 Cor. 6:19).

This only would I learn of you, Received ye the Spirit by the works of the law, or by the hearing of faith? (Gal. 3:2).

In whom ye also trusted, after that ye heard the word of truth, the gospel of your salvation: in whom also, after that ye believed, ye were sealed with that holy Spirit of promise (Eph. 1:13).

But after that the kindness and love of God our Saviour toward man appeared. Not by works of righteousness which we have done, but according to his mercy he saved us, by the washing of regeneration, and renewing of the Holy Ghost (Tit. 3:4, 5).

We noticed, in our last chapter, the difference between the *divine* and the *human* sides of Bible truth; we would, in this, advert to another distinction, of no less importance, that between Christ's work *for* us and the Holy Spirit's work *in* us; between the legal or substitutionary and the moral or curative.

This is not the distinction between a divine element and a human one, but between two elements which are both equally divine, yet each of them, in its own way, bearing very directly on the sinner.

The two things are sometimes put in another form, Christ for us, and Christ in us; the same, however, being the meaning in both cases; for 'Christ in us' (Col. 1:27) is also 'the Holy Spirit in us'; Christ having the Spirit without measure for himself (John 3:34) and for us according to our need. An indwelling Christ, and an indwelling Spirit are, though not the same thing, yet equivalent things. He who has the Son has the Spirit; nay, and the Father also (John 14:23).

Christ for us is our resting-place. Not works, nor feelings, nor love, even though these may be the creation of the Spirit in us; not these in any sense; no, nor yet faith whether as an act of our mind, or as the production of the Spirit, or as a substitute for righteousness; none of these can be our resting-place.

This great truth is well brought out in a correspondence between Melancthon and Brentius in the year 1531, which we translate and abridge. Brentius had been much perplexed on the subject of faith. It puzzled him. Christ justifies; faith justifies; how is this? Is faith a merit? Is it a work? Has it some justifying virtue in itself? Does it justify because it is the gift of God and the work of the Holy

Spirit? Perplexed with these questions, he wrote to
Melancthon and Luther. The replies of both are extant;
neither of them long; Luther's very short. They go straight
to the point and deserve to be quoted as clear statements
of the truth, and as specimens of the way in which these
men of might dealt with the burdened spirits of their time.

'I see,' writes Melancthon, 'what is troubling you about
faith. You stick to the fancy of Augustine, who, though
right in rejecting the righteousness of human reason,
imagines that we are justified by that fulfilling of the law
which the Holy Spirit works in us. So you imagine that
men are justified by faith, because it is by faith that we
receive the Spirit, that thereafter we may be able to be just
by that fulfilment of the law which the Spirit works. This
imagination places justification in our fulfilment of the
law, in our purity or perfection, although this renewal ought
to follow faith. But do you turn your eyes from that
renewal, and from the law altogether, to the promise and
to Christ, and think that it is on Christ's account that we
become just, that is, accepted before God, and that it is
thus we obtain peace of conscience, and not on account of
that renewal. For even this renewing is insufficient (for
justification). We are justified by faith alone, not because
it is a root, as you write, but because it apprehends Christ,
on account of whom we are accepted; this renewing,
although it necessarily follows, yet does not pacify the
conscience. Therefore not even love, though it is the
fulfilling of the law, justifies, but only faith; not because
it is some excellence in us, but only because it takes hold
of Christ; we are justified, not on account of love, not on
account of the fulfilling of the law, not on account of our
renewal, although these are the gifts of the Holy Spirit,

but on account of Christ; and him we take hold of by faith alone.

'Believe me, my Brentius, this controversy regarding the righteousness which is by faith is a mighty one, and little understood; and you can only rightly comprehend it by turning your eyes entirely away from the law, and from Augustine's idea about our fulfilling the law, and fixing them wholly upon the free promise, so as to see that it is on account of that promise, and for Christ's sake, that we are justified, that is, accepted and obtain peace. This is the true doctrine, and that which glorifies Christ and wonderfully lifts up the conscience. I endeavoured to explain this in my *Apology,* but on account of the misrepresentations of adversaries, could not speak out so freely as I do now with you, though saying the very same thing.

'When could the conscience have peace and assured hope, if we are not justified till our renewal is perfected? What is this but to be justified by the law, and not by the free promise? In that discussion I said that to ascribe our justification to love is to ascribe it to our own work; understanding by that, a work done in us by the Holy Ghost. For faith justifies, not because it is a new work of the Spirit in us, but because it apprehends Christ, on account of whom we are accepted, and not on account of the gifts of the Holy Spirit in us. Turn away from Augustine's idea, and you will easily see the reason of this; and I hope our *Apology* will somewhat help you, though I speak cautiously respecting matters so great, which are only to be understood in the conflict of the conscience. By all means preach law and repentance to the people, but let not this true doctrine of the gospel be overlooked.'

In the same strain writes Luther: 'I am accustomed, my Brentius, for the better understanding of this point, to conceive this idea, that there is no quality in my heart at all, call it either faith or charity; but instead of these I set Christ himself, and I say this is my righteousness, he is my quality and my formal righteousness as they call it, so as to free myself from looking into law or works; nay, from looking at Christ himself as a teacher or a giver. But I look at him as gift and as doctrine to me, in himself, so that in him I have all things. He says, "I am the way, and the truth, and the life"; he says not, I give thee the way and the truth, and the life, as if he were working on me from without. All these things *he* must be *in me;* abiding, living and speaking *in me,* not through me or to me; that we may be "the righteousness of God *in him*" (2 Cor. 5:21); not in love, nor in the gifts and graces which follow.'

To these letters Brentius replies, unfolding his conflicts to his beloved Philip. 'Is not faith itself a work?...Does not the Lord say, "This is the work of God that ye believe."... Justification then cannot be either by works or by faith...Is it so?... Therefore justification must be on account of Christ alone, and not the excellence of our works.... But how can all this be?... From childhood I had not been able to clear my thoughts on these points. Your letter and that of Luther showed me the truth.... Justification comes to us neither *on account of* our love nor our faith, but solely on account of Christ; and yet it comes *through* (by means of) faith. Faith does not justify as a work of goodness but simply as a receiver of promised mercy.... We do not *merit,* we only *obtain* justification.... Faith is but the organ, the instrument, the medium; Christ alone is the satisfaction and the merit. Works are not

satisfaction, nor merit, nor instrument; they are the
utterance of a justification already received by faith.'

Thus does the disciple expound the Master's letter, and
then adds some thoughts of his own. He fears lest, as
Popery perverted *love,* so the reformation might come to
pervert *faith*; putting it in the room of Christ, as a work or
merit or quality; *something in itself.* Having finished the
letter to his 'most beloved Philip,' and signed it 'thy
Brentius,' he starts another thought, and adds a postscript,
which is well worth the translating. 'Just as I was finishing
my letter, I remembered an argument of yours about works,
to the effect that if we are justified by *love, we can never
have assurance,* because we can never love as we ought.
In like manner I argue regarding *faith* as a work; if
justification come to us through faith as a work, or merit,
or excellence, we can never be assured about it, because
we can never believe as we ought.'

We have given some space to these extracts, because
the importance of the truth which they contain can hardly
be overrated. They not only exhibit the distinction between
Christ's work and the Spirit's work, but they do so with
special reference to that point at which they are so often
made to run into each other, to the darkening of many
minds and the confusion of all Reformation theology. For
how often did Luther reiterate that statement, 'Faith
justifies us, no, *not even as a gift of the Holy Ghost,* but
solely on account of its reference to Christ'...'faith does
not justify for its own sake, or because of any inherent
virtue belonging to it.' So long as this confusion exists; so
long as men do not distinguish between Christ's work and
the Spirit's work; so long as they lay any stress upon the
quality or quantity of their act of faith, there can be not

only no peace of conscience, but no progress in holiness; no bringing forth of good works.

Of this confusion, Arminianism, in its subtlest form, is the necessary offspring. For while men think to be justified by faith as a work, or as an act of their mind, or as a gift of the Spirit, they are seeking justification by something *inherent,* not by something *imputed;* and to deny that it is *inherent,* because *infused* into them by the Spirit, is simply to cheat themselves with a play upon words; and to cheat themselves all the more effectually, because professing to honour the Spirit by ascribing to him the infused quality or act, out of which they seek to extract their justification. In seeking justification or peace of conscience, from something wrought in them by the Spirit, they are seeking these from that which is confessedly imperfect, and which God never gave for such a purpose; nay, they are rejecting the perfect righteousness of the Substitute, and so preventing the possibility of their doing any acceptable works at all. For if 'the righteousness of the law can only be fulfilled in us' through our acceptance of the imputed righteousness of the Son of God, then there can be *no righteous thing done by us* till we have reached the position of men to whom the great truth of 'Christ for us,' Jehovah our righteousness,' has become the basis of all reconciliation with God. This form of error is the more subtle, because its victims are not walking in sin, but doing all manner of outward service, and exhibiting outward goodness in many forms, regarding which we shall only say that 'they are not pleasant to God'...and as 'they are not done *as God hath willed and commanded them to be done,* we doubt not but they have the nature of sin' (Art. XIII. Of the Church of England).

Some of the soundest Christian divines have left on record their complaint as to the mistakes in this matter of faith, prevailing in their day, and as to the charge of Antinomianism brought against those who, in stating justification, refuse to qualify the apostolic formula, 'to him that worketh not, but believeth'. Traill thus wrote, now nearly two centuries ago, 'If we say that *faith in Jesus Christ is neither work, nor condition, nor qualification* in justification, and that in its very act it is a renouncing of all things but the gift of grace, the fire is kindled; so that it is come to this, that he that will not be Antichristian must be called an Antinomian.'[1]

That we 'believe through grace', that faith is 'the gift of God' does not prove faith to be a work of ours, any more than Christ's raising of Lazarus proved resurrection to be a work of the dead man. The divine infusion of life in the one case, and the divine impartation of faith in the other, so far from showing that there must be a *work* in either, indicates very plainly that there could not be any such thing. The *work* comes *after* the believing, and as

---

1. How strongly does this same divine state the truth in another place. When addressing a perplexed inquirer he says, 'If he say that he cannot believe on Jesus Christ... you tell him *that believing on Jesus Christ is no work,* but a resting on Jesus Christ.' How sharply does he rebuke those who would mix up the *imputed* and the *infused;* 'they seem to be jealous lest God's grace and Christ's righteousness have too much room, and men's works too little in the business of justification.' See the whole of Traill's letter on 'Justification vindicated from the charge of Antinomianism'. An old anonymous writer, a little later than Traill, uses this expression: 'The Scriptures consider faith not as a work of ours, but set in opposition to every work, whether of body or mind – "to him that worketh not, but believeth." '

the fruit of it. 'Faith worketh by love,' that is, the believing soul shows its faith by works of love.

Yes, faith worketh; so also does love, so also does hope. These all *work*; and we read of 'the work of faith', that is, work to which faith prompts us; the 'labour of love', that is, the toil to which love impels us; the 'patience of hope', that is, the patience which hope enables us to exercise. But is faith a work because it worketh? Is love a toil because it toileth? Is hope patience because it makes us patient? Israel's looking to the brazen serpent was a *ceasing from all remedies,* and letting health pour itself into the body by the eye. Was the opening of the eye a work? The gospel does not command us to *do* anything in order to obtain life, but it bids us live by that which another has done; and the knowledge of its life-giving truth is not labour but *rest* – rest of soul – rest which is the root of all true labour; for in receiving Christ we do not work in order to rest, but we rest in order to work. In believing, we cease to work *for* pardon, in order that we may work *from* it; and what incentive to work or source of joy in working, can be greater than an ascertained and realised forgiveness.

That there are works done *before* faith we know; but we are assured that they profit nothing, 'for without faith it is impossible to please God.' That there are works done *after* faith we also know; and they are well pleasing to God, for they are the works of believing men. But, as to any *work* intermediate between these two, Scripture is silent; and against transforming faith into a work the whole theology of the Reformation protested, as either a worthless verbal quibble, or as the subtlest dregs of Popery.

Truly faith comes from God. The revelation which we believe, and the power by which we believe it, are both

divine. The Holy Spirit has written the Scriptures, and
sent them to us to be believed for salvation; faith cometh
by hearing, and hearing by the Word of God. He
quickens the dead soul that it may believe; and after it has
believed he comes in and dwells. Hence we are said to
receive the Spirit by 'the hearing of faith' (Gal. 3:2). He
opens our hand to receive the gift; and he places the gift in
our hand when thus opened by himself. Never let us forget
that while faith is the result of the Spirit's work in us, it is
as truly the *receiver* of himself as the indwelling Spirit;
and that in proportion to our faith will be the measure of
the Spirit we shall possess. This is another of the many
twofold truths or processes of Scripture; the Spirit works
to enable us to believe, and we in believing receive him
and all his gifts, in greater or less abundance, according to
our faith.

This twofold (See Appendix, Note 3), sometimes
threefold, aspect of a truth ought not to perplex us; still
less should it lead us to magnify one aspect at the expense
of the others, and to attempt a reconciliation of these by a
denial or evasion of one of them and a distortion of texts
that stand in our way. Let us admit the whole, and accept
the passages as they stand. Sometimes for example, our
renewal is connected with the Spirit (Tit. 3:5); sometimes
with Christ's resurrection (1 Pet. 1:3); sometimes with the
word of the truth (Eph. 1:13); and sometimes with faith
(John 1:12); sometimes it is spoken of as God's work (Ps.
51:10); sometimes as our own (Ezek. 18:31; Eph. 4:24);
sometimes as the effect of the gospel (1 Cor. 4:15). So is
it with conversion, with salvation, and with sanctification.
These are all spoken of in connection with God, with Christ,
with the Spirit, with the Word, with faith, with hope; and

each of these aspects must be studied, not evaded.[2]

But manifold as are these aspects, they all bear upon us personally; directly or indirectly affecting and carrying out our quickening, our healing, our joy, our comfort, and our holiness. There is no speculation in any of them; and it is truth, not opinion, that they present to us. Whatever amount of unreal religion may be in us, it is not because of any defect in the Word, any cloudiness in the gospel, any scantiness or straitness in the divine liberality, any lack in the fullness of him in whom it hath pleased the Father that all fullness should dwell. He has made provision for our being made like himself, and therefore he calls us to this likeness. The standard is high, but it does not admit of being lowered. The model is divine, but so is the strength given for conformity to it. Our responsibility to be holy is great, but not greater than the means provided for its full attainment.

In Christ dwells all the fullness of Godhead bodily. He has the Holy Spirit for us, and this Spirit he gives freely and plenteously; for that which we receive is 'grace, according to the measure of the gift of Christ'. The early saints were 'filled with joy and with the Holy Ghost' (Acts 13:52); and we are to be 'filled with the Spirit' (Eph. 5:18);

---

2. Calvin does not hesitate to speak of regeneration and repentance being the result of faith, 'regeneratio per fidem' (Inst. B. III.iii.1. See the whole third book). And Latimer writes, 'We be born again. How? Not by a mortal seed, but by an immortal. What is this immortal seed? The word of the living God. Thus cometh our new birth.' In stating one side of the truth these divines did not set aside the other. They taught renovation *through* the truth and *through* faith; and they also taught renovation *by* the power of the Holy Ghost. They taught man's need of the Spirit *in order to* faith, and they also proclaimed the gift of the Spirit *as the result* of faith.

for it is the Holy Ghost himself, not certain *influences* that are given unto us (Rom. 5:5). He 'falls' on us (Acts 8:16; 11:15); he is shed forth on us (Acts 2:33); he is poured out on us (Ezek. 39:29; Acts 10:45); we are 'baptized with the Holy Ghost' (Acts 11:16). He is 'the earnest of our inheritance' (Eph. 1:14); he 'seals' us (Eph. 1:13), imprinting on us the divine image and superscription; he 'teaches' (1 Cor. 2:13); he 'reveals' (1 Cor. 2:10); he 'strives' (Gen. 6:3); he 'sanctifies' (1 Cor. 6:11); he 'leads' (Rom. 8:14; Ps. 143:10); he 'instructs' (Neh. 9:20); he 'speaks' (1 Tim. 4:1; Rev. 2:7); he demonstrates (or proves) (1 Cor. 2:4), 'intercedes' (Rom. 8:26), 'quickens' (Rom. 8:11), 'gives utterance' (Acts 2:4); he 'creates' (Ps. 104:30); he 'comforts' (John 15:26); he 'sheds abroad the love of God in our hearts' (Rom. 5:5); he 'renews' (Tit. 3:5). He is the 'Spirit of holiness' (Rom. 1:4); the Spirit 'of wisdom and understanding' (Isa. 11:2; Eph. 1:17); the Spirit 'of truth' (John 14:17); the Spirit 'of knowledge' (Isa. 11:2); the Spirit 'of grace' (Heb. 10:29); the Spirit 'of glory' (1 Pet. 4:14); the Spirit 'of our God' (1 Cor. 6:11); the Spirit 'of the living God' (2 Cor. 3:3); the 'good' Spirit (Neh. 9:20); the Spirit 'of Christ' (1 Peter 1:11); the Spirit 'of adoption' (Rom. 8:15); the Spirit of life (Rev. 11:11); the Spirit of his Son (Gal. 4:6).

Such is the Holy Spirit by whom we are sanctified (2 Thess. 2:13); 'the eternal Spirit by whom Christ offered himself without spot to God' (Heb. 9:14). Such is the Holy Spirit by whom we are 'sealed unto the day of redemption' (Eph. 4:30); the Spirit who makes us his habitation (Eph. 2:22), who dwelleth in us (2 Tim. 1:14), by whom we are kept looking *to* and looking *for* Christ; by whom we are made to 'abound in *the hope*' (Rom. 15:13).

On the right receiving and entertaining of this heavenly
guest, much of a holy life depends. Let us bid him
welcome; not vexing, nor resisting, nor grieving, nor
quenching him; but loving him and delighting in his love;
('the love of the Spirit,' Rom. 15:30); that our life may be
a 'living' in the Spirit (Gal. 5:25); a 'walking' in the Spirit
(Gal. 5:16); a 'praying' in the Spirit (Jude 20); the life of
men, who, while distinguishing Christ's work *for* us and
the Spirit's work *in* us, and so preserving their conscious
pardon unbroken, yet do not separate the two by any
interval; but allowing both to do their work, 'follow peace
with all men, and holiness, without which no man can see
the Lord' (Heb. 12:14); keeping their hearts in 'the
fellowship of the Spirit' (Phil. 2:1), and delighting
themselves in 'the communion of the Holy Ghost' (2 Cor.
13:14).

The double form of expression, bringing out the mutual
or reciprocal indwelling of Christ and of the Spirit in us,
is worthy of special note. 'Christ in us' (Col. 1:27) is the
one side, we 'in Christ' is the other (2 Cor. 5:17; Gal.
2:20); the Holy Spirit in us (Rom. 8:9) is the one aspect,
we in the Spirit (Gal. 5:25) is the other. Nay, further, this
twofold expression is used of Godhead also, in these
remarkable words, 'Whosoever shall confess that Jesus is
the Son of God, God dwelleth in him, and he in God' (1
John 4:15).

It would seem as if no figure, however strong and full,
could adequately express the closeness of contact, the
nearness of relationship, the entire oneness into which we
are brought, in receiving the divine testimony to the person
and work of the Son of God. Are we not then most strongly
committed to a life of holiness, as well as furnished with

all the supplies needful for carrying it out? With such a fullness of strength and life at our disposal, what a responsibility is ours! 'What manner of persons ought we to be in all holy conversation and godliness!' And if to all this we add the *prospects* presented to us, the hope of the advent and the kingdom and the glory, we shall feel ourselves compassed on every side with the motives, materials, and appliances best fitted for making us what we are meant to be, 'a royal priesthood, an holy nation, a peculiar people,'[3] 'zealous of good works' here, and possessors of 'glory, and honour, and immortality' (Rom. 2:7) hereafter.

---

3. 1 Peter 2:9. It is remarkable that these words were first used regarding Israel (Exod. 19:5,6; Deut. 7:6), showing us that Old Testament saints did not stand on a lower level than New Testament ones. Most of the expressions used concerning the Church's privileges are Old Testament ones, borrowed from Israel's privileges. To the latter belonged the heavenly kingdom (Matt. 5:3; 8:11,12), the sonship (Exod. 4:22,23), the 'adoption, and the glory, and the promises' (Rom. 9:4).

CHAPTER 3

THE ROOT AND SOIL OF HOLINESS

But there is forgiveness with thee, that thou mayest be feared (Ps. 130:4).

Abide in me, and I in you. As the branch cannot bear fruit of itself, except it abide in the vine; no more can ye, except ye abide in me. I am the wine, ye are the branches: He that abideth in me, and I in him, the same bringeth forth much fruit: for without me ye can do nothing (John 15:4, 5).

I beseech you therefore, brethren, by the mercies of God, that ye present your bodies a living sacrifice, holy, acceptable unto God, which is your reasonable service (Rom. 12:1).

Who hath saved us, and called us with an holy calling, not according to our works, but according to his own purpose and grace, which was given us in Christ Jesus, before the world began (2 Tim. 1:9).

For the grace of God that bringeth salvation hath appeared to all men (Tit. 2:11).

This is a faithful saying, and these things I will that thou affirm constantly, that they which have believed in God might be careful to maintain good works. These things are good and profitable unto men (Tit. 3:8).

Who his own self bare our sins in his own body on the tree, that we, being dead to sins, should live unto righteousness; by those stripes ye were healed (1 Pet. 2:24).

Wherefore, beloved, seeing that ye look for such things, be diligent that ye may be found of him in peace, without spot, and blameless (2 Pet. 3:14).

And we have known and believed the love that God hath to us. God is love; and he that dwelleth in love dwelleth in God, and God in him. Herein is your love made perfect, that ye may have boldness in the day of judgment: because as he is, so are we in this world. There is no fear in love; but perfect love casteth out fear; because fear hath torment. He that feareth, is not made perfect in love. We love him, because he first loved us. If a man say, I love God, and hateth his brother, he is a liar: for he that loveth not his brother whom he hath seen, how can he love God whom he hath not seen? And this commandment have we from him, That he who loveth God love his brother also (1 John 4:16-21).

Every plant must have both soil and root. Without *both* of these there can be no life, no growth, no fruit.

Holiness must have these. The root is 'peace with God'; the soil in which that root strikes itself, and out of which it draws the vital sap, is the free love of God, in Christ Jesus our Lord. 'Rooted in love' is the apostle's description of a holy man. Holiness is not austerity nor gloom; these are as alien to it as levity and flippancy: nor is it the offspring of terror, or suspense, or uncertainty, but of *peace, conscious peace;* and this peace must be rooted in grace; it must be the consequence of our having ascertained, upon sure evidence, the forgiving love of God. He who would lead us into holiness must 'guide our feet into the way of peace' (Luke 1:79); must show us how we, 'being delivered out of the hands of our enemies, may serve God *without fear,* in holiness and righteousness, before him, all the days of our life' (Luke 1:74,75); and he who would do this must 'give us the knowledge of salvation, by the remission of sins;' must tell us how, through 'the tender mercy of our God, the day-spring from on high hath visited us, to give light to them that sit in darkness, and in the shadow of death' (Luke 1:78).

In carrying out the great work of making us *holy,* God speaks to us, as 'the God of *peace*' (Rom. 16:20); 'the very God of *peace*' (1 Thess. 5:23); as being himself 'our *peace*' (Eph. 2:14). That which we receive from Him, as such, is not merely '*peace* with God' (Rom. 5:1), but 'the *peace* of God' (Phil. 4:7), the thing which the Lord calls '*my* peace' (John 14:27), '*my* joy' (John 14:11). It is in connection with the exhortation, 'be perfect,' that the apostle sets down the gracious assurance, 'The God of *love and peace* shall be with you' (2 Cor. 13:11). 'These things I will that thou affirm constantly,' (says the apostle, speaking of 'the grace of God that bringeth salvation,' 'the kindness and love of God our Saviour,' the 'mercy of God,' 'justification by his grace', Tit. 2:11; 3:8), '*in order that* (such is the force of the Greek) they who have believed in God might be careful to maintain good works.'

In this 'peace with God' there is, of course, contained salvation, forgiveness, deliverance from the wrath to come. But these, though precious, are not terminating points; not ends, but beginnings; not the top but the bottom of that ladder which rests its foot upon the new sepulchre wherein never man was laid, and its top against the gate of the holy city. He, therefore, who is contenting himself with these, has not yet learned the true purport of the gospel, nor the end which God, from eternity, had in view when preparing for us such a redemption as that which he has accomplished for the sons of men, through his only begotten Son, 'who gave himself for us, that he might redeem us from all iniquity.'

Without these, holiness is impossible; so that we may say this at least, that it is through them that holiness is made practicable; for *the legal condition* of the sinner, as under wrath, stood as a barrier between him and the possibility of holiness. So long as he was under condemnation, the law prohibited the approach of everything that would make him holy. The law bars salvation, except on the fulfilment of its claims; so it bars holiness, until the great satisfaction to its claims has been recognised by the individual; that is, until he has believed the divine testimony to the atonement of the cross, and so been personally set free from condemnation. The law pronounces against the idea of holiness in an unforgiven man. It protests against it as an incongruity, and as an injury to righteousness. If, then, a pardoned man's remaining unholy seem strange, much more so a holy man remaining unpardoned. The sinner's *legal* position must be set to right before his *moral* position can be touched. Condition is one thing, character is another. The sinner's standing before God, either in favour or disfavour, either under grace or under wrath, must *first* be dealt with ere his inner renewal can be carried on. The judicial must precede the moral (See Appendix, Note 4).

Hence it is of pardon that the gospel first speaks to us; for the question of pardon must be settled before we proceed to others. The adjustment of the relationship between us and God is an indispensable preliminary, both on God's part and on ours. There must be friendship between us, ere *he* can bestow or *we* receive his indwelling Spirit; for, on the one hand, the Spirit cannot make his dwelling in the unforgiven; and on the other, the unforgiven must be so occupied with the one question of forgiveness that they are not at leisure to attend to anything till this has been finally settled in their favour. The man who knows that the wrath of God is still upon him, or, which is the same thing practically, is *not sure whether it has been turned away or not,* is really not in a condition to consider other questions, however important; if he has any true idea of the magnitude and terribleness of the anger of him who is a consuming fire.

The divine order then is first pardon, then holiness; first peace with God, and then conformity to the image of that God with whom we have been brought to be at peace. For as likeness to God is produced by beholding his glory (2 Cor. 3:18), and as we cannot look upon him till we know that he has ceased to condemn us, and as we cannot trust him till we know that he is gracious; so we cannot be transformed into his image till we have received pardon at his hands. Reconciliation is indispensable to resemblance; personal friendship must begin a holy life.

If such be the case, pardon cannot come too soon, even were the guilt of an unpardoned state not reason enough for any amount of urgency in obtaining it without delay. Nor can we too strongly insist upon the divine *order* above referred to; first peace, then holiness; peace as the foundation of holiness, even in the case of the chief of sinners.

Some do not object to a reputable man obtaining immediate peace; but they object to a profligate getting it at once! So it has always been; the old taunt is still on the lip of the modern Pharisee, 'He is gone to be guest with a man that is a sinner;' and the Simons of our day speak within themselves and say, 'This man, if he were a prophet, would have known who and what manner of woman this is that toucheth him, for she is a sinner' (Luke 7:39). But what then of Manasseh, and Magdalene, and Saul, and the woman of Sychar, and the jailor, and the men of

Jerusalem, whose hands were red with blood? Were they not trusted with a free and immediate peace? And did not the very essence and strength of the gospel's curative and purifying power lie in the freeness, the promptness, the certainty of the peace which it brought to these 'chief of sinners'?

'So you say you have found Christ, and have peace with God?' said one who claimed the name of 'Evangelical,' to a poor profligate that, only a few weeks before, had been drawn to the cross.

'I have, indeed,' said the poor man. 'I *have* found him, I *have* peace, and I know it.'

'*Know* it!' said the divine; 'and have *you* the presumption to tell me this? I have been a respectable member of a church for thirty years, and have not got peace nor assurance yet; and you, who have been a profligate most of your life, say that you have peace with God.'

'Yes, I have been as bad as a man can well be, but I have believed the gospel, and that gospel is good news for the like of me; and if I have no right to peace, I had better go back to my sins; for if I cannot get peace as I am, I shall never get it at all.'

'It's all a delusion,' said the other; 'do you think that God would give a sinner like you peace, and not give it to me who have been doing all I can to get it for so many years?'

'You are such a respectable man,' said the other, in unconscious irony, 'that you can get on without peace and pardon, but a wretch like me cannot; if my peace is a delusion, it cannot be a bad one, for it makes me leave off sin, and makes me pray and read my Bible; since I got it, I have turned over a new leaf.'

'It won't last,' said the other.

'Well, but it is a good thing while it does last; and it is strange to see the like of you trying to take from me the only thing that ever did me good; it looks as if you would be glad to see me going back to my old sins. You never tried to bring me to Christ; and, now when I have come to him, you are doing all you can to take me away. But I'll stick to him in spite of you.'

Some speak as if it were imperilling morality to let the sinner obtain immediate peace with God. If the peace be false, morality may be compromised by men pretending to the possession of a peace which is yet no peace. But, in that case, the evil complained of is the result of the *hollowness,* not the *suddenness,* of the peace, and can afford no ground for objecting to *speedy* peace, unless speedy peace is, of necessity, false, and unless the mere length of the process is security for the genuineness of the result. The existence of false peace is no argument against the true; and what we affirm is, that *true peace* can neither be too speedy nor too sure.

Others speak as if no sinner could be trusted with pardon till he has undergone a certain amount of preliminary mental suffering, more or less in duration and in intensity, according to circumstances. It would be dangerous to the interests of morality to let him obtain an immediate pardon; and especially to be sure of it, or to rejoice in it! If the man has been previously moral in life, they would not object to this; but they question the profligate's right to present peace, and protest against the propriety of it on grounds of subtle morality. They argue for delay, to give him time to improve before he ventures to speak of pardon; they insist upon a long season of preparatory conflict, years of sad suspense and uncertainty, in order to qualify the prodigal for his Father's embrace, and to prevent the unseemly spectacle of a sinner this week rejoicing in the forgiveness of his sins, who last week was wallowing in the mire. This season of delay, during which they would prohibit the sinner from assuring himself of God's free love, they consider the proper safeguard of a free gospel, and the needful guarantee for the sinner's future humility and holiness.

Is not, then, the position taken up by these men substantially that adopted by the Scribes, when they murmured at the Lord's gracious familiarity with the unworthy, saying, 'This man receiveth sinners, and eateth with them.' And is it not in great measure coincident with the opinion of Popish divines respecting the danger to morality from the doctrine of immediate justification through simple faith in the justifying work of Christ?[1]

The apostles evidently had great confidence in the gospel. They gave it fair play, and spoke it out in all its absolute freeness, as men who could trust it for its *moral influence,* as well as for its *saving power*; and who felt that the more speedily and certainly its good news were realized by the sinner the more would that moral influence come into play. They did not hide it, nor trammel it, nor fence it round with conditions, as if doubtful of the policy of preaching it freely. 'Be it known unto you,' they said,

---

1. When Bishop Gardiner, the Popish persecutor, lay dying in 1555, Day, bishop of Chichester, 'began to comfort him,' says Foxe, 'with words of God's promise, and free justification by the blood of Christ.' 'What,' said the dying Romanist, 'will *you* open that gap?' meaning that inlet of evil. 'To me and others in my case you may speak of it, but once open this window to the people, then farewell all good.'

'men and brethren, that through this man is preached unto
you the forgiveness of sins, and by him ALL THAT
BELIEVE ARE JUSTIFIED' (Acts 13:38). They had no
misgivings as to its bearings on morality; nor were they
afraid of men believing it too soon, or getting too
immediate relief from it. The idea does not seem to have
entered their mind, that men could betake themselves to
Christ too soon, or too confidently, or without sufficient
preparation. Their object in preaching it was, not to induce
men to commence a course of preparation for receiving
Christ, but to receive him at once and on the spot; not to
lead them through the long avenue of a gradually amended
life to the cross of the Sin-bearer; but to bring them at
once into contact with the cross, that so sin in them might
be slain, the old man crucified, and a life of true morality
begun. As the strongest motive to a holy life, they preached
the cross. They knew that 'The cross once seen is death to
every vice.' And *in the interests of holiness* they stood
and pleaded with men to take the proffered peace.

It is no disparagement to morality to say that good works
are not the way to Christ; it is no slighting of the sacraments
to say that they are not the sinner's resting place; so neither
is it any depreciation of devotion, or repentance, or prayer,
to say that they are not qualifying processes which fit the
sinner for approaching the Saviour, either as making the
sinner more acceptable or Christ more willing to receive.
Still less is it derogating from the usefulness or the
blessedness of these exercises, or feelings, to say that they
are often transformed into the refuges of self-righteousness,
pretexts which the sinner makes use of to excuse his guilt
in not at once taking salvation from the hands of Jesus.
We do not undervalue love because we say a man is not

justified by love, but by faith. We do not discourage prayer, because we preach that a man is not justified by prayer, but by faith. When we say that believing is not working, but a ceasing from work, we do not mean that the believing man is not to work; but that he is not to work for pardon, but to take it freely, and that he is to believe before he works, for works done before believing are not pleasing to God.

Is it the case that the sinner cannot be trusted with the gospel?

In one sense this is true. He cannot be trusted with anything. He abuses everything. He turns everything to bad account. He makes everything the minister of sin.

But if he cannot be trusted with the *gospel,* can he be trusted with the *law?* If he cannot be trusted with grace, can he be trusted with righteousness? He cannot be trusted with an immediate pardon, can he be trusted with a tardy one? He cannot be trusted with faith, can he be trusted with peace, can he be trusted with gloom and trouble? He cannot be trusted with assurance, can he be trusted with suspense; and will *uncertainty* do for him what *certainty* cannot?

That which he can, after all, best be trusted with is the gospel. He has abused it, he may abuse it, but he is less likely to abuse it than anything else. It appeals to deeper, stronger, and more numerous motives than all other things together.[2]

---

2. The teaching of some in the present day seems *fitted,* of others *intended,* to hinder assurance. Assurance, say some is impossible; not impossible, say others, but very hard of attainment; not only very hard, but very long of being reached, requiring at least some thirty or forty years of prayer and good works; very dangerous, say others,

Hence the apostles trusted the gospel with the sinner, and the sinner with the gospel, so unreservedly, and (as many in our day would say) unguardedly. 'To him that WORKETH NOT, BUT BELIEVETH, his faith is counted for righteousness,' was a bold statement. It is that of one who had great confidence in the gospel which he preached; who had no misgivings as to its unholy tendencies, if men would but give it fair play. He himself always preached it as one who believed it to be the power of God unto *holiness,* no less than unto *salvation.*

That this is the understanding of the New Testament, the 'mind of the Spirit,' requires no proof. Few would in words deny it to be so; only they state the gospel so timorously, so warily, so guardedly, with so many conditions, terms, and reservations, that by the time they have finished their statement, they have left no good news in that which they set out with announcing as 'the gospel of the grace of God.'

The more fully that the gospel is preached, in the grand old apostolic way, the more likely is it to accomplish the results which it did in apostolic days.

---

introducing presumption, and sure to end in apostasy. I confess I do not see how my being thoroughly persuaded that a holy God loves me with a holy love, and has forgiven me all my sins, has a tendency to evil (even though I may have reached that conclusion quickly). It seems, of all truths, one of the likeliest to make me holy, to kindle love, to stimulate to good works, and to abase all pride; whereas uncertainty in this matter enfeebles me, darkens me, bewilders me, incapacitates me for service, or, at the best, sets me a striving to work my way into the favour of God, under the influence of a subordinate and mercenary class of motives, which can do nothing but keep me dreading and doubting all the days of my life, leaving me, perhaps, at the close, in hopeless darkness.

The gospel is the proclamation of free love; the revelation of the boundless charity of God. Nothing less than this will suit our world; nothing else is so likely to touch the heart, to go down to the lowest depths of depraved humanity, as the assurance that the sinner has been *loved;* loved by God; loved with a righteous love; loved with a free love that makes no bargain as to merit, or fitness, or goodness. 'Herein is love, not that we loved God, but that he loved us!' As the Lord of the vineyard, after sending servant upon servant to the husbandmen in vain, sent at last his 'one son, his well-beloved' (Mark 12:6), so law having failed, God has despatched to us the message of his love, as that which is by far the likeliest to secure his ends. With nothing less than this free love will he trust our fallen race. He will not trust them with law, or judgement, or terror (though these are well in their place); but he will trust them with his love! Not with a stinted or conditional love; with half pardons, or an uncertain salvation, or a tardy peace, or a doubtful invitation, or an all but impracticable amnesty – not with these does he cheat the heavy laden; not with these will he mock the weary sons of men. He wants them to be holy, as well as safe; and he knows that there is nothing in heaven or earth so likely to produce holiness, under the teaching of the Spirit of holiness, as the knowledge of his own free love. It is not law, but 'the love of Christ,' that constraineth! 'The strength of sin is the law' (1 Cor. 15:56); neither yet 'under the law' (Rom. 6:14); but 'under grace,' that we should 'serve in newness of Spirit, and not in the oldness of the letter.'[3]

---

3. Thus Calvin writes: 'Consciences obey the law, not constrained by the necessity of law, but, being made free from the yoke of law, they

But so many (it is said) of those who were awakened under the preaching of this very free gospel have gone back, that suspicions arise as to whether it may not be the *ultra-freeness* of the gospel preached that has produced the evil. It is suggested that, had the gospel been better guarded both before and behind, we should have seen fewer falls and less inconsistency. To this our answer is ready. Multitudes 'went back' from our Lord, yet no one could blame his preaching. There were many grievous corruptions in the early church, yet we do not connect these with apostolic doctrine. Our Lord's parable of the sower implies that, however good the seed might be, and careful the sower, there would be stony-ground hearers, and thorny-ground hearers, going a certain length and then turning back. So that the backslidings complained of are such as the apostles experienced; such as our Lord led us to anticipate, under the preaching of his own full gospel.

Further than this, however, we add, that, while the

---

voluntarily obey the will of God. They are in perpetual terror as long as they are under the dominion of the law, and are never disposed to obey God with delighted eagerness unless they have first received this liberty' (Inst. III. xix.4). 'Not to be under the law (says Luther) is to do good and abstain from evil, not through the compulsion of law, but by free love and with gladness.' 'If any man ask me (says Tyndale), seeing faith justifies me, why I work, I answer, love compelleth me; for as long as my soul feeleth what love God hath shewed me in Christ, I cannot but love God again, and his will and commandments, and of love work them; nor can they seem hard to me' (Pref. to *Exodus*). 'When faith hath bathed a man's heart in the blood of Christ, it is so mollified that it generally dissolves into tears of godly sorrow; so that if Christ but turn and look upon him, oh then, with Peter he goes out and weeps bitterly. And this is true gospel mourning; this is right evangelical repenting' (Fisher's *Marrow of Modern Divinity*).

preaching of a guarded gospel may lead to no backslidings, it will accomplish no awakenings; so that the question will come to be this, Is it not better to have some fallings away when many are aroused, than to have no fallings away, *because none have been shaken?* The question as to what kind of teaching results in fewest backslidings is, no doubt, an important one; but still it is subordinate to the main one, What preaching produces, upon the whole, the most conversions, and brings most glory to God? Apostasies will occur in the best of churches, bringing with them scandal to the name of Jesus, and suspicion of the gospel as the cause of all the evil.

But is this a new thing in the earth? Is it not one of the things that strikingly identify us with Corinth, and Sardis, and Laodicea? A minister who has never had his heart wounded with apostasy, who knows nothing of the disappointment of cherished hopes, has too good reason to suspect that there is something sadly wrong and that the reason of there being no backslidings in his flock, is because death is reigning. Where all is silence or sleep; where the preaching does not shake and penetrate, there will be fewer fallings away; but the reason is, that there was nothing to fall away from.

'Where are your converts now?' was the question put to a faithful minister who had had to mourn the fall of some who once 'ran well.' 'Just where they were; the true still holding fast, the untrue showing themselves.' It was meant as a taunt; but it was a taunt which might have been cast at apostles. It was a taunt which carried comfort with it, as reminding the faithful minister of apostolic disappointments, and so bringing him into fellowship with

Paul himself; and as recalling the blessed fact that though some had fallen, more were standing.[4]

Some ask the question: Is it not a suspicious sign of your gospel, that any of the hearers of it should say, May we continue in sin that grace may abound? On the contrary, it is a safe sign of it. Had it not been very like Paul's gospel, it would not have led to the same inquiry with which the apostle's preaching was met. The restricted, guarded, conditional gospel, which some give us, as the *ultimatum* of their good news, would have suggested no such thought as that which the sixth chapter of the Romans was written to obviate. The argument of the apostle, in such a case, becomes unmeaning and superfluous; and hence that very statement which prompts some caviller to ask the question, 'Shall we sin because we are not under the law but under grace?' (Rom. 6:15) is not at all unlikely to be the authentic Pauline gospel, the genuine doctrine of apostolical antiquity.

---

4. The whole Galatian Church had lapsed into error and sin. How does the apostle cure the evil.? By fencing or paring down the gospel, and making it less free? No, but by reiterating its freeness; nay, stating it more freely than ever. How *free does* he represent it in the epistle to that church! Hence Luther chose it for comment, as the one best suiting himself.

CHAPTER 4

STRENGTH AGAINST SIN

Because the law worketh wrath; for where no law is, there is no transgression (Rom. 4:15).

Knowing this, that our old man is crucified with him, that the body of sin might be destroyed, that henceforth we should not serve sin. For he that is dead is freed from sin. Now if we be dead with Christ, we believe that we shall also live with him: knowing that Christ, being raised from the dead, dieth no more; death hath no more dominion over him. For in that he died, he died unto sin once: but in that he liveth, he liveth unto God. Likewise reckon ye also yourselves to be dead indeed unto sin, but alive unto God through Jesus Christ our Lord. Let not sin therefore reign in your mortal body, that ye should obey it in the lusts thereof. Neither yield ye your members as instruments of unrighteousness unto sin: but yield yourselves unto God, as those that are alive from the dead, and your members as instruments of righteousness unto God. For sin shall not have dominion over you: for ye are not under the law, but under grace. What then? shall we sin, because we are not under the law, but under grace? God forbid. Know ye not, that to whom ye yield yourselves servants to obey, his servants ye are to whom ye obey; whether of sin unto death, or of obedience unto righteousness? But God be thanked, that ye were the servants of sin, but ye have obeyed from the heart that form of doctrine which was delivered you. Being then made free from sin, ye became the servants of righteousness (Rom. 6:6-18).

O wretched man that I am! who shall deliver me from the body of this death? I thank God, through Jesus Christ our Lord. So then, with the mind I myself serve the law of God; but with the flesh the law of sin (Rom. 7:24-25).

For the law of the Spirit of life in Christ Jesus hath made me free from the law of sin and death. For what the law could not do, in that it was weak through the flesh, God, sending his own Son in the likeness of sinful flesh, and for sin, condemned sin in the flesh (Rom. 8:2-3).

But thanks be to God, which giveth us the victory through our Lord Jesus Christ. Therefore, my beloved brethren, be ye steadfast, unmoveable, always abounding in the work of the Lord, forasmuch as ye know that your labour is not in vain in the Lord (1 Cor. 15:56-57).

For I through the law am dead to the law, that I might live unto God (Gal. 2:19).

For as many as are of the works of the law, are under the curse: for it is written, Cursed is every one that continueth not in all things which are written in the book of the law to do them. But that no man is justified by the law in the sight of God, it is evident: for, The just shall live by faith. And the law is not of faith, but, The man that doeth them shall live in them. Christ hath redeemed us from the curse of the law, being made a curse for us: for it is written, Cursed is every one that hangeth on a tree: That the blessing of Abraham might come on the Gentiles through Jesus Christ: that we might receive the promise of the Spirit through faith (Gal. 3:10-14).

Forasmuch then as Christ hath suffered for us in the flesh, arm yourselves likewise with the same mind: for he that hath suffered in the flesh hath ceased from sin; That he no longer should live the rest of his time in the flesh to the lusts of men, but to the will of God (1 Pet. 4:1-2).

For whatsoever is born of God overcometh the world: and this is the victory that overcometh the world, even our faith (1 John 5:4).

Men live in sin, and yet they have the secret thought that they ought not to live, so that they ought to get rid of it. Even those that have not the law, in this respect 'are a law unto themselves;' for 'the *work* of the law (that is, *each thing* the law enjoins us to do) is written in their hearts;

their conscience also bearing witness, and their thoughts struggling with each other, either accusing or excusing' (Rom. 2:15. See Greek).

The groan of humanity, as well as the groan of creation, by reason of sin, has been deep and long. Not loud always; often an under-tone; oftener drowned in laughter; but still terribly real.

Sin as *disease,* infectious and hereditary; sin as *guilt,* inferring divine condemnation and doom, has been acknowledged; and along with the acknowledgement, the sad consciousness has existed that the race was not made for sin, and that man himself, not God, had wrought the wrong. Men in all ages, and of all religions, have, in some poor way, put in their protest against sin, 'knowing the judgement of God, that they which commit such things are worthy of death' (Rom. 1:32). The fallen sons of Adam, though haters of God and of his law (Rom. 1:30), have thus unconsciously become witnesses against themselves, and unwittingly taken the side of God and of his law.

All through the ages has this struggle gone on, between the love and the dread of sin, the delight in lust and the sense of degradation because of it; men clasping the poisoned robe, yet wishing to tear it off; their life steeped in the evil, yet their words so often lavished upon the good.

With much warmth did the ancient pagan wisdom of Greece and Rome utter itself against vice; with deep pathos at times describing the conflict with self, and the victory over the unruly will and the irregular appetite. But it suggested no remedy, and promised no power in aid. It could only say, 'Fight on.' Philosophy was helpless in its encounters with human evil, and in its sympathies with earthly sorrow. It looked on, and spoke many a true word;

but it wrought no cure; it healed no wounds; it rooted out no sin. It was the exhibition of weakness, not of power; the mere cry of human helplessness (See Appendix, Note 5).

Romish devotees, with fastings and flagellations, in addition to earnest words, have tried to extirpate the wrong and nourish the right. Groping after righteousness, yet not knowing what righteousness is, nor how it comes to us, they have built themselves up in *self*-righteousness. Professing to seek holiness, without understanding its nature, they have snared themselves in delusions which bring no purity.

Bent, as they say, upon 'mortifying the flesh;' falsely identifying 'the flesh' with the mere body; and working upon the theology which teaches that it is the body which ruins the soul, they lay great stress on weakening and macerating the corporeal frame, not knowing that they are thus feeding sin, fostering pride, making the body less fit to be the helpmeet of the soul, and thereby producing unholiness of the darkest type in the eye of God. By rules of no gentle kind; by terror, by pain, by visions of death and the grave, by pictures of a fiercely flaming hell, by the denial of all certainty in pardon, they have sought to terrify or force themselves into goodness. By long prayers, by bitter practices of self-denial, by slow chaunts at midnight or early morn in dim cathedrals, by frequent sacraments, by deep study of old fathers, by the cold of wintry solitudes, by multiplied deeds of merit and will-worship, they have thought to expel the demon, and to eradicate 'the ineradicable taint of sin.'

But success has not come in this way. The enterprise was a high but a fearful one; and the men knew not how terrible it was. They had quite under-rated the might of the enemy, while over-estimating their own. The resources of the two sides were indeed unequal. Not Leonidas against the myriads of Persia, nor the old Roman Three who held the bridge against the Etruscan host, could be compared to this. It might seem but the feeble aberrations of one poor human heart that they were dealing with; but they knew not what these indicated; what the power of a human will is for evil; what is man's hostility to God; what is the vitality of sin; what is the exasperating tendency of naked law, and the elasticity of evil under legal compression; what is the tenacity of man's resistance to goodness and to the law of goodness; what all these together must be when fostered from beneath, and backed by the resources of hell.

In all this there is not one thought of *grace* or divine free-love; no recognition of forgiveness as the root of holiness. Man's philosophy and man's religion have never suggested this. It would seem as if man could not trust himself with this, and could not believe that God would trust him with it. He has no idea of barriers against sin, save in the shape of walls, and chains, and bars of iron; of torture, and threats and wrath. On these alone he relies. He is slow to learn that all legal deterrents are in their very nature *irritants,* with no power to produce or enforce anything but a constrained externalism. The interposition of forgiving love, in absolute completeness and freeness, is resisted as an encouragement to evil-doing; and, at the most, grace, only in a very conditional and restricted form, is allowed to come into play. The dynamics of grace have never been reduced to a formula; they are supposed incapable of being so set down. That God should act in any other character than as the rewarder of the deserving and the punisher of the undeserving; that he should go down into the depths of a human heart, and there touch springs which were reckoned inaccessible or perilous to deal with; that his gospel should throw itself upon something nobler than men's fear of wrath, and *begin* by proclaiming pardon as the first step to holiness; this is so incredible to man, that, even with the Bible and the cross before his eyes, he turns away from it as foolishness.

Nevertheless this is 'the more excellent way;' nay, the true and only way of getting rid of sin. Forgiveness of sins, in believing God's testimony to the finished propitiation of the cross, is not simply indispensable to a holy life, in the way of removing terror and liberating the soul from the pressure of guilt, but of imparting an impulse, and a motive, and a power which nothing else could do. Forgiveness *at the end or in the middle;* a partial forgiveness, or an uncertain forgiveness, or a grudging forgiveness, would be of no avail; it would only tantalize and mock; but a complete forgiveness, presented in such a way as to carry its own certainty along with it to every one who will take it at the hands of God; this is a *power* in the earth, a power against self, a power against sin, a power over the flesh, a power for holiness, such as no amount of suspense or terror could create.

It is to this that our Lord refers, once and again, when dealing with the Pharisees, those representatives of a human standard of goodness as contrasted with a divine. How deep the significance of such statements as these:- 'When they had nothing to pay, he frankly forgave them both' (Luke 7:42); 'her sins, which are many, are forgiven' (Luke 7:47); 'the lord of that servant was moved with compassion and loosed him, and forgave him the debt'

(Matt. 18:27); 'neither do I condemn thee, go and sin no more' (John 8:11); 'I came not to call the righteous, but sinners to repentance' (Luke 5:32); 'the Son of man is come to seek and to save that which was lost' (Luke 19:10); 'God so loved the world that he gave his only begotten Son' (John 3:16); 'I came not to judge the world, but to save the world' (John 12:47). It is to this also that the apostles so often refer in their discourses and epistles: 'Who his own self bare our sins in his own body on the tree, that we, being dead to sins, should live unto righteousness' (1 Pet. 2:24); 'through this man is preached unto you the forgiveness of sins' (Acts 13:38); 'God commendeth his love toward us, in that, while we were yet sinners, Christ died for us' (Rom. 5:8); 'herein is love, not that we loved God, but that he loved us' (1 John 4:10); 'we love him because he first loved us' (1 John 4:19). To this, also, all the prophets had given witness; thus, 'I will pardon all their iniquities' (Jer. 33:8); 'there is forgiveness with thee that thou mayest be feared' (Ps. 130:4); 'as far as the east is from the west, so far hath he removed our transgressions from us' (Ps. 103:12); 'I, even I, am he that blotteth out thy transgressions for mine own sake, and will not remember thy sins' (Isa. 43:25).

Yet it is not a question of motives and stimulants merely that is indicated in all this. It is one of release from bondage; it is the dissolution of the law's curse. Under law and its curse, a man works for self and Satan; 'under grace' he works for God. It is forgiveness that sets a man a-working for God. He does not work in order to be forgiven,[1] but because he has been forgiven; and the consciousness of

---

1. 'Non ut vivat sed quia vivit,' says Turrentine (Instit. Theol. Xi.24.7).

his sin being pardoned, makes him long more for its entire removal than ever he did before.

An unforgiven man cannot work. He has not the will, nor the power, nor the liberty. He is in chains. Israel in Egypt could not serve Jehovah. 'Let my people go, that they may serve me,' was God's message to Pharaoh (Exod. 8:1); first liberty, then service.

A forgiven man is the true worker, the true law-keeper. He *can,* he *will,* he *must* work for God. He has come into contact with that part of God's character which warms his cold heart. Forgiving love constrains him. He cannot but work for him who has removed his sins from him as far as the east is from the west. Forgiveness has made him a free man, and given him a new and most loving Master. Forgiveness received freely from the God and Father of our Lord Jesus Christ acts as a spring, an impulse, a stimulus of divine potency. It is more irresistible than law, or terror, or threat. A half forgiveness, an uncertain justification, a changeable peace, may lead to careless living and more careless working; may slacken the energy and freeze up the springs of action, (for it shuts out that aspect of God's character which gladdens and quickens); but a *complete and assured pardon* can have no such effect. This is 'the truth which is after godliness' (Titus 1:1). Its tendencies towards holiness and consistency of life are marvellous in their power and certainty. *Irrepressible* we may truly call the momentum thus imparted to the soul; a momentum which owes its intensity to the *entireness and sureness* of the pardon; a momentum on which some, in their ignorance of Scripture, as well as of the true deep springs of human action, would fasten their drag of doubt and uncertainty, lest what they call the interests of morality should be compromised. As if men could be made unholy by knowing *certainly* with what a holy love they have been freely loved; or made holy by being kept in suspense as to their own personal reconciliation with God. As if pardon, doled out in crumbs or drops, and even these so cautiously held out, or rather held back, that a man can hardly ever be sure of having them, were more likely to be fruitful in good works than a pardon given at once, and given in such a way as to be sure even to the chief of sinners; a pardon worthy, both in its greatness and its freeness, of the boundless generosity of God.[2] (See Appendix, Note 6).

---

2. It would be well for many if they would study Mr. Robert Haldane's *Exposition of the Epistle to the Romans*, especially the second volume. It is a noble protest against the meagre teaching of many so-called Protestants on the subject of justification by faith. Its faithful condemnation of the false, and bold vindication of the true may be reckoned too 'decided,' perhaps 'extreme,' by 'advanced' theologians; but the Church of God, in these days of diluted doctrine, will be thankful for such an assertion of Reformation theology. His strong point is his elucidation of the Apostle's statements as to the believer's being 'dead to sin,' which he shows to have 'no reference to the *character* of believers, but exclusively to their *state* before God, *as the ground on which their sanctification is secured,*' (vol. ii. p.22). To be 'dead to sin' is a *judicial* or *legal,* not a *moral* figure. It refers to our release from condemnation, our righteous disjunction from the claim and curse of law. This, instead of giving licence to sin, is the beginning and root of holiness.

CHAPTER 5

THE CROSS AND ITS POWER

I have blotted out, as a thick cloud, thy transgressions, and, as a cloud, thy sins: return unto me; for I have redeemed thee (Isa. 44:22).

Seventy weeks are determined upon thy people, and upon thy holy city, to finish the transgression, and to make an end of sins, and to make reconciliation for iniquity, and to bring in everlasting righteousness, and to seal up the vision and prophecy, and to anoint the Most Holy (Dan. 9:24).

In that day there shall be a fountain opened to the house of David, and to the inhabitants of Jerusalem, for sin and for uncleanness (Zech. 13:1).

And he that taketh not his cross, and followeth after me, is not worthy of me (Matt. 10:38).

But we preach Christ crucified, unto the Jews a stumblingblock, and unto the Greeks foolishness.... But of him are ye in Christ Jesus, who of God is made unto us wisdom, and righteousness, and sanctification, and redemption (1 Cor. 1:23, 30).

And they that are Christ's have crucified the flesh with the affections and lusts (Gal. 5:24).

Before I can live a Christian life, I must be a Christian man. Am I such? I ought to *know* this. Do I know it, and, in knowing it, know whose I am, and whom I serve? Or is my title to the name still questionable, still a matter of anxious debate and search? (See Appendix, Note 7).

If I am to *live* as a son of God, I must *be* a son, and I must *know* it, otherwise my life will be an artificial imitation, a piece of barren mechanism, performing certain excellent movements, but destitute of vital heat and force. Here many fail. They try to *live* like sons, in order to *make* themselves sons, forgetting God's simple plan for attaining sonship at once, 'As many as *received him,* to them gave he power to become the sons of God' (John 1:12).

The faith of many amongst us is, after all, but a trying to believe, their repentance but a trying to repent; and, in so doing, they but use words which they have learned from others. It is not the love of holiness that actuates them, but (at best) the love of the love of holiness; it is not the love of God that fills them, but the love of the love of God.[1]

God's description of a Christian man is clear and well-defined. It has about it so little of the vague and wide that one wonders how any mistake should have arisen on this point, and so many dubious, so many false claims put in.

A Christian is one who 'has tasted that the Lord is gracious' (1 Peter 2:3); who has been 'begotten again unto a lively hope' (1 Peter 1:3); who 'has been quickened together with Christ' (Eph. 2:5); 'made partaker of Christ' (Heb. 3:14); 'partaker of the divine nature' (2 Pet. 1:4);

---

1. In many, the love of the truth is but partial. In some, it is but the *sentimental* side of the truth that is loved; in others the *logical;* in others, the *traditional*; in others, the *pictorial*; in others, the *poetical;* in others, the *beautiful.* Very far short does this fall of what the apostle calls 'receiving the love of the truth that they might be saved' (2 Thess. 2:10); nay, it is not inconsistent with the 'strong delusion' and the 'belief of the lie,' against which he warns us (verse 11). It is often out of such men and such materials that are formed the 'wells without water,' the 'clouds carried about with a tempest,' the 'trees twice dead,' the 'wandering stars to whom is reserved the blackness of darkness for ever' (2 Peter 2:17, Jude 13).

who 'has been delivered from a present evil world' (Gal. 1:4).

Such is God's description of one who has found his way to the cross, and is warranted in taking to himself the Antiochian name of 'Christian,' or the apostolic name of 'saint.' Of good about himself, previous to his receiving the record of the free forgiveness, he cannot speak. He remembers nothing loveable that could have recommended him to God; nothing fit that could have qualified him for the divine favour, save that he *needed* life. All that he can say for himself is, that he 'has known and believed the love that God hath to us' (1 John 4:16); and, in believing, has found that which makes him not merely a *happy,* but a *holy* man. He has discovered the fountain-head of a holy life.

Have I then found my way to the cross? Then I am safe. I *have* the everlasting life. The first true touch of that cross has secured for me the eternal blessing. I am in the hands of Christ, and none shall pluck me thence (John 10:28).

The cross makes us whole; not all at once indeed, but it does the work effectually. Before we reached it we were not 'whole,' but broken and scattered, nay, without a centre toward which to gravitate. The cross forms that centre, and, in so doing it draws together the disordered fragments of our being; it '*unites* our heart' (Ps. 86:11), producing a wholeness or unity which no object of less powerful attractiveness could accomplish;[2] a wholeness or unity

---

2. '*Colligis nos*' (thou gatherest us together), says Augustine, (Conf.i.3); and again '*Colligens* me a dispensione in qua frustratim discissus sum; dum ab uno te aversus, in multa evanui' (Conf. Xi.1).

which, beginning with the individual, reproduces itself on a larger scale, but with the same centre of gravitation, in the Church of God.

Of spiritual health, the cross is the source. From it there goes forth the 'virtue' (δυναμις, the power, Luke 6:19) that heals all maladies, be they slight or deadly. For 'by *his* stripes we are *healed*' (Isa. 53:5); and in *him* we find 'the tree of life,' with its healing leaves (Rev. 22:2). Golgotha has become Gilead, with its skilful physician and its 'bruised' balm (Jer. 8:22). Old Latimer says well regarding the woman whom Christ cured, 'she believed that Christ was *such a healthful man* that she should be sound as soon as she might touch him.' The 'whole head was sick, and the whole heart was faint' (Isa. 1:5); but now the sickness is gone, and the vigour comes again to the fainting heart. The look, or rather the object looked at, has done its work. (Isa. 45:22); the serpent of brass has accomplished that which no earthly medicines could effect. Not to us can it now be said, 'Thou hast no *healing* medicines' (Jer. 30:13), for the word of the great Healer is, 'I will bring *health and cure*; yea, I will *cure* them, and will reveal unto them the abundance of peace and truth' (Jer. 33:6). Thus it is by 'the abundance of that *peace and truth*,' revealed to us in the cross, that our cure is wrought.

The cure is not perfected in an hour. But, as the sight of the cross begins it, so does it complete it at last. The pulses of new health now beat in all our veins. Our whole being recognises the potency of the divine medicine, and our diseases yield to it.

Yes, the cross heals. It possesses the double virtue of killing sin and quickening holiness. It makes all the fruits of the flesh to wither, while it cherishes and ripens the fruit of the Spirit, which is 'love, joy, peace, longsuffering, gentleness, goodness, faith, meekness, temperance' (Gal. 5:22). By this the hurt of the soul is not 'healed slightly,' but truly and thoroughly. It acts like the fresh balm of southern air to one whose constitution the frost and damp of the far north had undermined. It gives new tone and energy to our faculties, a new bent and aim to all our purposes, and a new elevation to all our hopes and longings. It gives the death-blow to self, it mortifies our members which are upon the earth, it crucifies the flesh with its affections and lusts. Thus, looking continually to the cross, each day, as at the first, we are made sensible of the restoration of our soul's health; evil loosens its hold, while good strengthens and ripens.

It is not merely that we 'glory in the cross' (Gal. 6:14), but we draw *strength* from it. It is the place of *weakness,* for there 'Christ was crucified through *weakness*' (2 Cor. 13:4); but it is, notwithstanding, the fountain-head of *power* to us; for as, out of death, came forth life, so out of weakness came forth strength. This is strength, not for one thing, but for everything. It is strength for activity or for endurance, for holiness as well as for work. He that would be holy or useful, must keep near the cross. The cross is the secret of power, and the pledge of victory. With it we fight and overcome. No weapon can prosper against it, nor enemy prevail. With it we meet the fightings without as well as the fears within. With it we war the good warfare, we wrestle with principalities and powers, we 'withstand' and we 'stand' (Eph. 6:12,13); we fight the good fight, we finish the course, we keep the faith (2 Tim. 4:7).

Standing by the cross we become imitators of the crucified one. We seek to be like him – men who please not themselves (Rom. 15:3); who do the Father's will, counting not our life dear unto us, who love our neighbours as ourselves, and the brethren as he loved us; who pray for our enemies; who revile not again when reviled; who threaten not when we suffer, but commit ourselves to him that judgeth righteously; who live not to ourselves, and who die not to ourselves; who are willing to be of 'no reputation,' but to 'suffer shame for his name,' to take the place and name of 'servant,' nay, to count 'the reproach of Christ greater riches than the treasures in Egypt' (Heb. 11:26). 'Forasmuch, then, as Christ hath suffered for us in the flesh, arm yourselves with the same mind; for he that hath suffered in the flesh, hath ceased from sin,' (has 'died to sin,' as in Romans 6:10), 'that he no longer should live the rest of his time in the flesh to the lusts of men, but to the will of God' (1 Peter 4:1,2).

Standing by the cross, we realize the meaning of such a text as this: 'Our old man is (was) crucified with him, that the body of sin might be destroyed, that henceforth we should not serve sin' (Rom. 6:6); where the crucifixion of our old man, the destruction of the body of sin, and deliverance from the bondage of sin, are so strikingly linked to one another, and linked, all of them, to the cross of Christ. (See Appendix, Note 8). Or we read the meaning of another: 'I am (have been) crucified with Christ: nevertheless I live; yet not I, but Christ liveth in me: and the life which I now live in the flesh, I live by the faith of the Son of God, who loved me, and gave himself for me' (Gal. 2:20). Here *the one Paul* (not two Pauls, or two persons), speaks throughout, as completely identified with Christ and his cross. It is not one part of Paul in this clause and another in that; it is the one whole Paul throughout, who is crucified, dies, lives! Like Isaac, he has been 'received from the dead in a figure;' and as Abraham would, after the strange Moriah transaction, look on Isaac as given back from the dead, so would Jehovah reckon and treat this Paul as a risen man! Isaac would be the same Isaac, and yet not the same; so Paul is the same Paul, and yet not the same! He has passed through something which alters his state legally, and his character morally; he is new. Instead of the first Adam, who was of the earth earthly, he has got the last Adam, who is the Lord from heaven, for his guest; 'Christ liveth in him;' 'I live, yet not I, but Christ liveth in me,' (just as he says, 'Yet not I, but the grace of God in me'); and so he lives the rest of his life on earth, holding fast his connection with the crucified Son of God and his love. Or again, we gather light upon that text, 'They that are Christ's have crucified the flesh with the affections and lusts' (Gal. 5:24); and that, 'God forbid that I should glory, save in the cross of our Lord Jesus Christ, by whom the world is crucified unto me and I unto the world' (Gal. 6:14). (See Appendix, Note 9).

Standing by the cross, we realize the *death* of the Surety, and discover more truly the meaning of passages such as these: 'Ye are *dead* (ye died), and your life is hid with Christ in God' (Col. 3:3); 'Ye *died* with Christ from the rudiments of the world' (Col. 2:20); his death (and yours with him) dissolved your connection with these. 'If one died for all, then were all dead (all died); and he died for all, that they who live should not henceforth live unto themselves, but unto him who died for them and rose again' (2 Cor. 5:14, 15). 'To this end Christ both died and rose, and revived, that he might be Lord both of the dead and living' (Rom. 14:9). 'He that is dead (has died) is freed (justified) from sin, (*i.e.* he has paid the penalty); now, if we be dead with Christ (or since we died with Christ), we believe that we shall also live with him, knowing that Christ being (having been) raised from the dead, dieth no more (he has no *second* penalty to pay, no second death to undergo, Heb. 9:27,28), death hath no more dominion over him (Rom. 6:7, 8); for in that he died, he died unto sin once (his death finished his sin-bearing work once for all); but in that he liveth, he liveth unto God; likewise reckon ye also yourselves to be dead indeed unto sin, but alive unto God, through Jesus Christ our Lord; let not sin therefore reign in your mortal body (*even* in your *body,* Rom. 12:1), that ye should obey it in the lusts thereof' (Rom. 6:9-12).

There is something peculiarly solemn about these passages. They are very unlike, both in tone and words, the light speech which some indulge in, when speaking of the gospel and its forgiveness. Ah, this is the language of one who has in him the profound consciousness that severance from sin is one of the mightiest, as well as most blessed, things in the universe! He has learned how deliverance from condemnation may be found, and all legal claims against him met. But, more than this, he has learned how the grasp of sin can be unclasped, how its serpent-folds can be unwound, how its impurities can be erased, how he can defy its wiles and defeat its strength – HOW HE CAN BE HOLY! This is, to him, of discoveries one of the greatest and most gladdening. Forgiveness itself is precious, chiefly as a step to holiness. How any one, after reading statements such as those of the apostle, can speak of sin, or pardon, or holiness without awe, seems difficult to understand. Or how any one can feel that the forgiveness which the believing man finds at the cross of Christ, is a release from the obligation to live a holy life, is no less incomprehensible.

It is true that sin remains in the saint; and it is equally true that this sin does not bring condemnation back to him. But there is a way of stating this which would almost lead to the inference that watchfulness has thus been rendered less necessary; that holiness is not now so great an urgency; that sin is not so terrible as formerly. To tell a sinning saint that no amount of sin can alter the perfect standing before God into which the blood of Christ brings us, may not be technically or theologically incorrect; but this mode of putting the truth is not that of the Epistle to the Romans or Ephesians; it sounds almost like, 'Continue in sin because grace abounds;' and it is not Scriptural language. The apostolic way of putting the point is that of 1 John 1:9–2:1: 'If we confess our sins, he is faithful and just to forgive us our sins…. If any man sin, we have an advocate with the Father, Jesus Christ the righteous.'

Thus, then, that which cancels the curse provides the purity. The cross not only pardons, but it purifies. From it there gushes out the double fountain of peace and holiness. It heals, unites, strengthens, quickens, blesses. It is God's wing under which we are gathered, and 'he that dwelleth in the secret place of the Most High shall abide under the shadow of the Almighty' (Ps. 91:1).

But we have *our* cross to bear, and our whole life is to be a bearing of it. It is not Christ's cross that we are to carry; that is too heavy for us, and besides, it has been done once for all. But *our* cross remains, and much of a Christian life consists in a true, honest, decided bearing of it. Not indeed to be nailed to it, but to take it up and carry it – this is our calling. To each of us a cross is presented when we assume the name of Christ. Strange will it be if we refuse to bear it; counting it too heavy or too sharp, too much associated with reproach and hardship. The Lord's words are very uncompromising, 'If any man will come after me, let him deny HIMSELF, and take up *his cross* and follow me' (Matt. 16:24). Our refusal to do this may contribute not a little to our ease and reputation here; but it will not add to the weight of the glory which the resurrection of the just shall bring to those who have confessed the Master, and borne his shame, and done his work in an evil world.

With the 'taking up of the cross DAILY' (Luke 9:23), our Lord connects the denial of *self* and the following of him. *He* 'pleased not *himself;*' neither must we, for the servant is not above his master. He did not his own will; neither must we, for the servant is not above his Lord. If we endure no hardness, but are self-indulgent, self-sparing men, how shall we be followers of him? If we grudge labour, or sacrifice, or time, or money, or our good name, are we remembering his example? If we shrink from the weight of the cross, or its sharpness, or the roughness of the way along which we have to carry it, are we keeping his word in mind, 'Ye shall drink indeed of my cup, and be baptized with the baptism that I am baptized with?' (Matt. 20:23).

The cross on which we are crucified with Christ, and the cross which we carry, are different things, yet they both point in one direction, and lead us along one way. They both protest against sin, and summon to holiness. They both 'condemn the world,' and demand separation from it. They set us upon ground so high and so unearthly, that the questions which some raise as to the expediency of conformity to the world's ways are answered as soon as they are put, and the sophistries of the flesh, pleading on behalf of gaiety and revelry, never for a moment perplex us. The kingdom is in view, the way is plain, the cross is on our shoulders, and shall we turn aside after fashions and frivolities, and pleasures, and unreal beauties, even were they all as harmless as men say they are? It may seem a small thing now to be a lover of pleasure more than a lover of God, but it will be found a fearful thing hereafter, when the Son of Man comes in his glory, and all his holy angels with him. It may seem a possible thing just now, by avoiding all extremes and all *thoroughness,* either in religion or in worldliness, to conjoin both of these, but in the day of the separation of the real from the unreal, it will be discovered to have been a poor attempt to accomplish an impossibility; a failure; a failure for eternity, a failure as complete as it is disastrous and remediless. Egypt and Canaan cannot coalesce; Babylon and Jerusalem can never be one. These are awful words, 'We are of God, and the whole world lieth in wickedness'; and surely the Holy Spirit meant what he said, when he enjoined, 'Love not the world, neither the things that are in the world; if any man love the world, the love of the Father is not in him' (1 John 2:15).

The cross, then, makes us *decided* men. It brings both our *hearts* and our *wills* to the side of God. It makes us feel the cowardice as well as guilt of *indecision,* bidding us be bold and stable, 'holding faith and a good conscience;' all the more because the wide 'liberality' of modern free thinking has confounded scepticism with candour, and recognises in religious indifference a virtue and a grace.

Not to take any side strongly is no evidence of a large soul or a great purpose. It is generally an indication of littleness.

The furrows drawn by a firm hand are strongly and deeply drawn. It is no surface work; soil and subsoil are turned over with a decision which implies that, if the work is worth doing at all, it is worth doing well. The man of true purpose and strong mind handles his plough resolutely, from end to end of the longest furrow, till the whole field be wrought. Thus do men of true will and aim proceed, both in belief and action. Having put their hand to the plough, they do not so much as *look* back.

The thoughts and purposes of men bear the impress of the mind from which they emerge, as much in their *decision,* as in their general character. As earth's streams are *decided* in their flow, and owe the measure of their decision to the elevation of the mountain-range down whose steeps they pour, so is it with the opinions and actings of men. Decision is no proof of weakness; it is not bigotry, nor intolerance, nor ignorance, though it has sometimes been the emanation of these, and identified with them.

Every thing in the Bible is decided; its statements of fact, its revelations of truth, its condemnation of error, its declarations respecting God and man, respecting our present and our future. Its characters are decided men – Abraham, Moses, Joshua, Elijah, Paul. It speaks always with authority, as expecting to be implicitly credited. It reckons on our receiving its teaching, not doubtfully but certainly; and it leaves us only the alternative of denying its whole authenticity, or of accepting its revelations, without a qualification and without a subterfuge. To excuse ourselves for doubt and indecision, and oscillation of faith, by pointing to differences of creed, is to suggest either that Scripture is not infallible, or that it is not intelligible. The Bible is God's direct revelation, *to each man* into whose hand it comes, and, for the reception of all that it contains, each man is responsible, though all his fellows should reject it. The judgment day will decide who is right; meanwhile it is to God and not to man that we are to listen. For the understanding of God's revelation, each one is accountable. If it can be proved that the Bible is so uncertainly written as to render diversity of thought a necessity, or so obscurely expressed as to keep men in ignorance, then, when the day of reckoning comes, the misled man will have opportunity of substantiating his charges against God, and of claiming deduction from his penalty, on the plea of the ambiguity of the statute. Meanwhile we are responsible for *decision* – decision in thought and action, on every point on which the Holy Spirit has written; and it is not likely that the Spirit of wisdom and love, in writing a book for us, would write so darkly as to be unintelligible, or should give such an uncertain sound that no man could be sure as to which, out of a score of meanings suggested by man, was the genuine.

Man's usual thought is, that the want of explicitness in the Bible is the cause of diversity of opinion, and that a little more fullness of statement and clearness of language would have prevented all sects and confusion. The answer to this is twofold: (1) That greater fullness would have only opened new points of divergence and variance, so that, instead of a hundred opinions, we should, in that case, have had a thousand; (2) That the real cause of all the divergence and unsettlement is to be found in man's *moral* state; that there is not a veil upon the Bible, but scales on human eyes; and that, were that spiritual imperfection entirely removed, the difficulty would be, not how to believe, but how *not* to believe; and the wonder would be how it was possible for us to attach more than one meaning to words so significant and simple.

CHAPTER 6

THE SAINT AND THE LAW

The law of the LORD is perfect, converting the soul: the testimony of the LORD is sure, making wise the simple: The statutes of the LORD are right, rejoicing the heart: the commandment of the LORD is pure, enlightening the eyes: The fear of the LORD is clean, enduring for ever: the judgments of the LORD are true and righteous altogether. More to be desired are they than gold, yea, than much fine gold; sweeter also than honey and the honeycomb. Moreover, by them is thy servant warned: and in keeping of them there is great reward (Ps. 19:7-11).

My son, forget not my law; but let thine heart keep my commandments (Prov. 3:1).

My son, keep my words, and lay up my commandments with thee. Keep my commandments, and live; and my law as the apple of thine eye. Bind them upon they fingers, write them upon the table of thine heart. Say unto wisdom, Thou art my sister; and call understanding thy kinswoman (Prov. 7:1-4).

But this shall be the covenant that I will make with the house of Israel; After those days, saith the LORD, I will put my law in their inward parts, and write it in their hearts; and will be their God, and they shall be my people. And they shall teach no more every man his neighbour, and every man his brother, saying, Know the LORD: for they shall all know me, from the least of them unto the greatest of them, saith the LORD; for I will forgive their iniquity, and I will remember their sin no more (Jer. 31:33, 34).

Therefore all things whatsoever ye would that men should do to you, do ye even so to them: for this is the law and the prophets (Matt. 7:12).

O wretched man that I am! who shall deliver me from the body of this death (Rom. 7:22).

That the righteousness of the law might be fulfilled in us, who walk not after the flesh, but after the Spirit (Rom. 8:4).

Owe no man any thing, but to love one another: for he that loveth another hath fulfilled the law. For this, Thou shalt not commit adultery, Thou shalt not kill, Thou shalt not steal, Thou shalt not bear false witness, Thou shalt not covet; and if there be any other commandment, it is briefly comprehended in this saying, namely, Thou shalt love thy neighbour as thyself (Rom. 13:8-10).

Children, obey your parents in the Lord: for this is right. Honour thy father and mother, which is the first commandment with promise, that it may be well with thee, and thou mayest live long on the earth (Eph. 6:1-3).

If ye fulfil the royal law, according to the scripture, Thou shalt love thy neighbour as thyself, ye do well (James 2:8).

And whatsoever ye ask, we receive of him, because we keep his commandments, and do those things that are pleasing in his sight (1 John 3:22).

And this is love, that we walk after his commandments. This is the commandment, That, as ye have heard from the beginning, ye should walk in it (2 John 6)

'God imputeth righteousness without works,' says the Holy Spirit, speaking through Paul (Rom. 4:6); and he who is in possession of this righteousness is 'a blessed man.' (See Appendix, Note 10).

This righteousness is at once divine and human; 'the righteousness of God' (Rom. 1:17); the 'righteousness of him who is our God and Saviour' (2 Peter 1:1; see Greek); the righteousness of him whose name is 'Jehovah, our righteousness,' (Jer. 23:6). It is 'righteousness without the law' (Rom. 3:21); yet righteousness which has all along been testified to by 'the law and the prophets'. It is the

'righteousness which is of faith' (*i.e.* which is got by
believing, Rom. 10:6), 'without the deeds of the law'
(Rom. 3:28), yet arising out of a fulfilled law. It is the
righteousness, not of the Father or of Godhead, but of the
Son, the Christ of God, the God-man; of him who, by his
obedient life and death, magnified the law and made it
honourable.

Thus, then, on believing the divine testimony
concerning this righteousness, we are no longer 'under
the law, but under grace' (Rom. 6:14); we are 'dead to the
law by the body (the crucifixion, or crucified body) of
Christ'; we are 'delivered from the law, that being dead
(viz., the law) wherein we were held' (Rom. 7:6).

It appears, then, that the gospel does not change the
law itself, for it is holy, and just, and good; that grace
does not abate the claims nor relax the penalties of law.
The law remains the same perfect code, with all its old
breadth about it, and all its eternal claims. For what is the
purport of the gospel, what is the significance of grace? Is
it perfect obedience on our part to the perfect law? That
would be neither gospel nor grace. Is it perfect obedience
to a relaxed, a less strict law? That would be the ruin of
law on the one hand, and the exaction of an obedience on
the other, which no sinner could render. Is it imperfect
obedience to an unrelaxed, unmodified law? That would
be salvation by *sin,* not by *righteousness.* Or, lastly, is it
imperfect obedience to a relaxed and imperfect law? That
would be the destruction of all government, the dishonour
of all law; it would be the setting up 'the throne of iniquity,'
and 'framing mischief by law' (Ps. 94:20). The demand
of the law is *perfection.* Between *everything* and *nothing*
the Bible gives us our choice. If we are to be saved by the

law, it must be *wholly by the law*; if not wholly by the law, it must be wholly without the law.

But while it is clear that the law is not changed, and cannot be changed, either in itself or in its claims, it is as clear that our relations to the law, and the law's relations to us, has altered, upon our believing on him who is 'the end (or fulfilling) of the law for righteousness to every one that believeth'. If, indeed, the effect of Christ's death had been to make what is called, 'evangelical obedience to a milder law,' our justifying righteousness, then there would be a change in the law itself, though not in our relation to it, which would in that case remain the same, only operating on a lower scale of duty. But if the end of Christ's life and death be to substitute his obedience for ours entirely, in the matter of justification, so that his doings meet every thing in law that our doings should have met, then the relationship between us and law is altered; we are placed upon a new footing in regard to it, while it remains unchanged and unrelaxed.

What, then, is the new relationship between us and law, which faith establishes?

There are some who speak as if in this matter there is the mere breaking up of the old relationship, the cancelling of the old covenant, without the substitution of anything new. They dwell on such texts as these: 'Not under the law,' 'delivered from the law,' affirming that a believing man has nothing more to do with law at all. They call that 'imperfect teaching' which urges obedience to law in the carrying out of a holy life; they brand as bondage the regard to law which those pay who, studying Moses and the prophets, and specially the psalms of him who had tasted the blessedness of the man to whom the Lord imputeth

righteousness without works (Ps. 32:1), are drinking into
the spirit of David, or more truly, into the spirit of the
greater than David, the only begotten of the Father, who
speaks, in no spirit of bondage, of the laws and statutes
and judgements and commandments of the Father.

Our old relationship to law (so long as it continued)
made justification by law a necessity. The *doing* was
indispensable to the *living,* so long as the law's claims
over us personally were in force. We strove to obey, in
order that we might live; for this is *law's* arrangement, the
legal order of things; and so long as this order remained
there was no hope. It was impossible for us to 'obey and
live'; and as the law could not say to us, 'live and obey,' it
could do nothing for us. Only that which could reverse
this order in our case, which could give *life in order to
obedience,* would be of any service to us. This the gospel
steps in to do. Not first obedience and then life, but first
life and then obedience.

This argues no weakness or imperfection in the law.
For if any law could have given life, this law would have
done it (Gal. 3:21). But law and life, in the case of the
sinner, are incompatible. It is the very perfection of the
law that makes life impossible under it, unless in the case
of entire and ceaseless obedience, without a flaw. 'By the
law is the knowledge of sin;'[1] and where sin is, law
proclaims death, not life.

So long, then, as the old relationship continued between

---

1. This text does not apply merely to the operation of law upon the
sinner's conscience, convincing him of his guilt; it points also to the
instruction which law gives us regarding sin all the days of our life.
We learn sin and its details from the law; we learn the penalty
elsewhere.

us and law; or, in the apostle's words, so long as we were 'under law,' there was nothing but condemnation and an evil conscience, and the fearful looking for of judgement. But with the change of relationship there came pardon and liberty and gladness. 'Christ hath redeemed us from the curse of the law, being made a curse for us' (Gal. 3:13); and so we are no longer under law, but under grace. The law is the same law, but it has lost its hold of us, its power over us. It cannot cease to challenge perfect obedience from every being under heaven, but to us its threat and terror are gone. It can still say 'Obey,' but it cannot now say 'Disobey and perish.'

Our new relationship to the law is that of Christ himself to it. It is that of men who have met all its claims, exhausted its penalties, satisfied its demands, magnified it, and made it honourable. For our faith in God's testimony to Christ's surety-obedience has made us one with him. The relation of the law to him is its relation to us who believe in his name. His feelings towards the law ought to be our feelings. The law looks on us as it looks on him; we look on the law as he looks on it. And does not he say, 'I delight to do thy will, O my God; yea, THY LAW is within my heart' (Ps. 40:8).

Some speak as if the servant were greater than the Master, and the disciple above his Lord; as if the Lord Jesus honoured the law, and his people were to set it aside; as if he fulfilled it for us, that we might not need to fulfil it; as if he kept it, not that we might keep it, but that we might not keep it, but something else in its stead, they know not what.

The plain truth is, we must either keep it or break it. Which of these men ought to do, let those answer who speak of a believer having nothing more to do with law. There is no middle way. If it be not a saint's duty to keep the law, he may break it at pleasure, and go on sinning because grace abounds.

The word *duty* is objected to as inconsistent with the liberty of forgiveness and sonship. Foolish and idle cavil! What is *duty?* It is the thing which is *due by me to God;* that line of conduct which *I owe to God.* And do these objectors mean to say that, because God has redeemed us from the curse of the law, therefore we *owe* him nothing, we have no *duty* now to him? Has not redemption rather made us *doubly debtors?* We *owe* him more than ever; we owe his holy law more than ever; more honour, more obedience. Duty has been *doubled,* not *cancelled,* by our being delivered from the law; and he who says that *duty* has ceased, because deliverance has come, knows nothing of duty, or law, or deliverance. The greatest of all debtors in the universe is the redeemed man, the man who can say, 'The life that I live in the flesh I live by the faith of the Son of God, who loved me, and gave himself for me.' What a strange sense of gratitude these men must have who suppose that because love has cancelled the penalties of law, and turned away its wrath, therefore reverence and obedience to that law are no longer *due*! Is *terror,* in their estimation, the only foundation of duty; and when love comes in and terror ceases, does duty become a bondage?

No, they may say; but there is something higher than duty, there is privilege; it is that we contend for.

I answer, the privilege of what? Of obeying the law? *That* they cannot away with; for they say they are no longer under law, but under grace. What privilege, then? Of imitating Christ? Be it so. But how can we imitate him whose life was one great law-fulfilling, without keeping the law? What privilege, again we ask? Of doing the will of God? Be it so. And what is law but the revealed will of God? And has our free forgiveness released us from the privilege of conformity to the revealed will of God?

But what do they mean by thus rejecting the word duty, and contending for that of privilege? Privilege is not something distinct from duty, nor at variance with duty, but it is duty *and something more;* it is duty influenced by higher motives; duty uncompelled by terror or suspense. In privilege the *duty* is all there; but there is something superadded, in shape of motive and relationship, which exalts and ennobles duty. It is my duty to obey government; it is my privilege to obey my parent. But in the latter case is duty gone because privilege has come in? Or has not the loving relationship between parent and child only intensified the duty, by superadding the privilege, and sweetening the obedience by the mutual love? 'The love of Christ *constraineth.*' That is something more than both duty and privilege added.

Let men who look but at one side of a subject say what they will, this is the truth of God, that we are liberated from the law just in order that we may keep the law; we get the 'no condemnation' in order that 'the *righteousness of the law* may be fulfilled in us' (Rom. 8:4); we are delivered from 'the mind of the flesh', which is enmity to God and not subject to his law, on purpose that we may be *subject to his law* (Rom. 8:7), that we may '*delight in the law* of God after the inward man' (Rom. 7:22); nay, that we may 'with the mind *serve the law* of God' (Rom. 7:25); that we may be 'doers of *the law*' (James 4:11). These objectors may speak of obedience to the law as bondage,

or of the law itself being abolished to believers; here are
the words of the Holy Ghost; the law of God is just the
law of God; that very law which David loved, and in which
David's Son delighted; and what delighting in it, serving
it, doing it, are, it would be well for such men meekly and
lovingly to learn.

'Do we make void the law by faith? God forbid: yea,
we *establish* the law' (Rom. 3:31); that is, we set it on a
firmer basis than ever. That law, 'holy, and just, and good,'
thus doubly established, is now *for* us, not *against* us. Its
aspect towards us is that of friendship and love, and so we
have become 'the *servants* of righteousness' (Rom. 6:18),
'yielding our members *servants* to righteousness' (Rom.
6:19). We are not men delivered from service, but delivered
from one kind of service, and by that deliverance
introduced into another, 'that we should *serve* in newness
of spirit, and not in the oldness of the letter' (Rom. 7:6);
as 'the Lord's *freemen*' (1 Cor. 7:22), yet Christ's *servants*
(1 Cor. 7:22). Thus, obligation, duty, service, obedience,
still remain to the believing man, though no longer
associated with bondage and terror, but with freedom and
gladness and love. The law's former bearing on us is
altered, and, with that, the *nature* and spirit of the service
are altered, but the service itself remains, and the law which
regulates that service is confirmed, not annulled.

Some will tell us here that it is not *service* they object
to, but service regulated by *law.* But will they tell us what
is to regulate service, if not law? *Love,* they say. This is a
pure fallacy. Love is not a *rule* but a *motive.* Love does
not tell me *what* to do; it tells me *how* to do it. Love
constrains me to do the will of the beloved one; but to
know what that will is I must go elsewhere. The law of

our God is *the will* of the beloved one, and were that expression of his will withdrawn, love would be utterly in the dark; it would not know what to do. It might say, I love my Master, and I love his service, and I want to do his bidding, but I must know *the rules of his house,* that I may know *how* to serve him. Love without law to guide its impulses would be the parent of will-worship and confusion, as surely as terror and self-righteousness, unless upon the supposition of an inward miraculous illumination, as an equivalent for law. Love goes to the law to learn the divine *will,* and love delights in the law, as the exponent of that will; and he who says that a believing man has nothing more to do with law, save to shun it as an old enemy, might as well say that he has nothing to do with the will of God. For the divine law and the divine will are substantially one, the former the outward manifestation of the latter. And it is '*the will* of our Father which is in heaven' that we are to do (Matt. 7:21); so proving by loving obedience what is that 'good, and acceptable, and perfect *will of God'* (Rom. 12:2). Yes, it is 'he that doeth *the will* of God that abideth for ever' (1 John 2:17); it is to 'the *will of God* that we are to live' (1 Peter 4:2); 'made perfect in every good work *to do his will'* (Heb. 13:21); and 'fruitfulness in every good work' springs from being 'filled with the knowledge of *his will'* (Col. 1:9-10).

As to the oneness between divine *will* and divine *law,* I need only quote the words of him who came to fulfil the law: 'Lo, I come: in the volume of the book it is written of me, I delight to do *thy will,* O my God: yea, *thy law* is within my heart' (Ps. 40:7-8; Heb. 10:7).

If *law* be not *will,* what is it? And if will has not uttered itself in law, in what has it spoken? *Truth* is the utterance of the divine *mind,* but law is the utterance of the divine *will.* When a father teaches his child, we see simply *mind* meeting *mind;* but when he commands or gives rules, we see *will* meeting *will.* When parliament publishes reports of proceedings, or the like, there is simply the expressions of its *mind;* when it passes an act, there is the declaration of its *will.*

I ask attention to this, the real meaning of law, because it is the key to the solution of the question before us. That question is really not so much concerning the *law* of God as concerning his *will*; and the theology which would deny the former would set aside the latter. Conformity to the will of God can only be carried out by observance of his law, for we know his will only through his law.

I do not see how a crooked will is to be straightened unless by being brought into contact with 'the perfect *will* of God'; nor do I see how that will is to be brought to bear upon us, for the rectification of our will, unless by the medium of the revealed law. *Will* must be brought to bear upon *will,* unless some miraculous power be put forth in us apart altogether from the truth of God; and he who affirms this may also affirm that peace is to be dropped into us apart from the gospel of peace. The divine volition, embodied in a force or power which we call gravitation, rules each motion of the unconscious planets, and this same divine volition or will, embodied in intelligible law, is that which regulates the movements of our conscious wills, straightening them and keeping them straight, though without wrong done to their nature or violation of their true freedom.

Should it be said that will and law are now *embodied in* CHRIST; and that it is to this model that we are to look,

I ask, What do we see in Christ? The fulfiller of the law.
He is the embodiment and perfection of law-fulfilling. We
cannot look at him without seeing the perfect law. God
has given us these two things in these last days, the law
and the living model; but was the living model meant to
supersede the law? Was it not to illustrate and enforce it?
We see the law now, not merely in the statute-book, but in
the person of the King himself. But is the statute-book
thereby annihilated, and its statutes made void? Were
Christ's expositions of the law in the fifth, sixth and
seventh chapters of Matthew intended to over-rule or
abrogate the law itself? No; but to show its breadth and
purity. And when he thus expounded the law, did he say
to his disciples, 'But *you* have nothing to do with this law;
it is set aside for all that shall believe in my name.' Did he
not liken to a wise man every one who should hear these
sayings of his and do them (Matt. 7:24); nay, did he not
say, 'Think not that I am come to destroy *the law* or the
prophets. I am not come to destroy, but to fulfil
....Whosoever, therefore, shall break *one of these least
commandments, and shall teach men so,* he shall be called
least in the kingdom of heaven' (Matt. 5:17-19). Now one
would think that this should settle the question. For the
Lord is speaking of the law and its commandments, lesser
and greater, and he is speaking of it as binding on them
who are heirs of the kingdom of heaven.

Should it be said that it is only exemption from
obligation to the moral law or ten commandments that is
pleaded for, and not the law or will of God in general, I
answer, the ten commandments are the summary or
synopsis of God's will as to the regulation of man's life;
and every other part of the Bible is in harmony with this

moral law.[2] So that exemption from compliance with *any Bible statute*, or from the obligation of submitting ourselves to *any Bible truth*, might be pleaded for as properly as exemption from the law. For the law cannot be cut out of the Bible and set aside by itself, while all else remains in force. Either all must go or none.

If the objection is to the use of the word 'law', or 'commandment', as implying bondage, I answer, obedience to law is true liberty; perfect obedience to perfect commandments is perfect liberty. And there must be some dislike of the law's strictness where this dislike of obligation to it is felt; nay, there must be ignorance of gospel, as well as law, in such a case, ignorance of that very redemption from the curse of the law for which the objectors profess such zeal, ignorance of the complete 'righteousness without the law' which we have in Christ. I am persuaded of this, that where there is this shrinking from the application of law as our rule of life, there is a shrinking *from perfect conformity to the will of God*; nay, more, there is *unbelief in the gospel,* the want of a *full*

---

2. Besides, the ten commandments were for *redeemed* Israel. The Sinaitic code began with redemption, 'I am the LORD thy God which brought thee out of the land of Egypt, and out of the house of bondage' (Exod. 20:2; Deut. 5:6). Israel was *to keep them because they were redeemed;* 'the LORD thy God redeemed thee, *therefore I command* thee this day' (Deut. 15:15). Redemption forms a new obligation to law-keeping, as well as puts us in a position for it. And was it not to Sinai and its burnings that the apostle referred when he said, 'We receiving a kingdom which cannot be moved, let us have grace, whereby we may serve God acceptably with reverence and godly fear, *for our God is a consuming fire*' (Heb. 12:28, 29). Some would, perhaps, call this legality and bondage, a motive unfit to be addressed to a saint.

consciousness of the perfect forgiveness which the belief of that gospel brings; for were there this full consciousness of pardon, there would be no dread of law, no shrinking from Sinai's thunders, no wish to be exempted from the broadest application of Sinai's statutes. In all Antinomianism, whether practical or theological, there is some mistake both as to law and gospel.

But why object to such words as law and commandment and obedience? Does not the apostle speak of 'the *law* of the Spirit of life'? Does he not say, 'This is his *commandment,* that we should believe on the name of his Son Jesus Christ' (1 John 3:23)? And is not 'the *new* commandment' said to be only a repetition of 'the *old* commandment,* which we have heard from the beginning' (1 John 2:7)? And does he not speak of '*obedience* unto righteousness' (Rom. 6:16) and of '*obedience* to the faith'? (Rom. 1:5).

When the apostle is exhorting Christians in the 12th and 13th of the Romans, is he not giving precepts and laws? Nay, and does he not found his exhortations on the ten commandments? 'For this thou shalt not kill, thou shalt not steal, thou shalt not covet; and if there be *any other commandment,* it is briefly comprehended in the saying, thou shalt love thy neighbour as thyself. Love worketh no ill to his neighbour, therefore love is the *fulfilling of the law*' (Rom. 13:9,10). The ten commandments are here presented as our guide and rule, which guide and rule *love* enables us to follow; for the apostle does not say, 'love is exemption from the law, or love is the abrogation of the law,' but 'love is the fulfilling of the law.' Love does not supersede law, nor release us from obedience to it; it enables us to obey. Love does not make stealing or

coveting, or any such breach of law, *no sin in a Christian,*
which would seem to be the meaning which some attach
to this passage; but it so penetrates and so constrains us
that, not reluctantly or through fear but right joyfully, we
act towards our neighbour in all things, great and small,
as the law bids us do. Yes, Christ 'hath redeemed us from
the curse of the law', but certainly not from the law itself;
for that would be to redeem us from a divine rule and
guide; it would be to redeem us from that which is 'holy
and just and good'.

In other epistles the same reference occurs to the ten
commandments as the basis of a true and righteous life.
Thus, in speaking of the family relationship, the apostle
introduces the moral law as the foundation of obedience:
'Children, obey your parents in the Lord: for this is right;
honour thy father and mother, which is the first
commandment with promise; that it may be well with thee,
and thou mayest live long on the earth' (Eph. 6:1-3), where,
writing to those who are *in the Lord,* and not Jews but
Gentiles, he demands obedience and honour in the name
of *the fifth commandment.* Yet surely, if any duty might
have been left to the impulses of Christian love, without
reference to law, it would be that of a believing child to its
parent. Was the apostle, then, a legalist when he referred
the Ephesians to the law as a rule of life? Did he not know
that they were 'not under the law but under grace'?

In the Epistle of James we find similar appeals to the
moral law as the rule of Christian life. That he is speaking
of the ten commandments is evident, for he quotes *two of
them* (2:11) as specimens of what he calls the law. This
law he bids his Christian brethren 'look into' (1:25),
'continue in' it (1:25), 'fulfil' it (2:8), 'keep' it (2:10), be

'doers' of it (4:11). And this law he calls 'the law of liberty' (2:12); nay, 'the perfect law of *liberty*' (1:25), carrying us back to the Psalmist's experience, 'I will walk at *liberty*, for I seek thy precepts' (Ps. 119:45); for law is bondage only to the unforgiven; all true obedience is liberty, and all true liberty consists in obedience to law. This law, moreover, the apostle so delights in that he calls it 'the royal law' (2:8), the 'perfect law' (1:25), pronouncing those blessed who are 'not forgetful hearers, but *doers* of the work' (1:25). Had this apostle forgotten that we were 'not under the law, but under grace'? But he was writing to Jews, some say. Yes, but to *believing Jews,* just as Paul was when writing to 'the Hebrews' and when writing to 'the Romans' also (Rom. 2:17-29). And do men mean to say that there is one gospel for the Jew and another for the Gentile; that the Jew is still 'under the law, and *not under grace*; and that in Christ Jesus all nations of men are not entirely ONE' (Eph. 2:14-22; 1 Cor. 12:12-13; Gal. 3:28).

If the objection to the believer's use of the law be of any weight, it must apply to *everything in the form of precept*; for the reasons given against our having anything to do with the moral law are founded upon its *preceptive* or *commanding* character. The law, in itself, is admitted to be good, and breaches of it are sin, as when a man steals or lies; but then, the form in which it comes, of *do* or *do not,* makes it quite unsuitable for a redeemed man! Had it merely said 'stealing is wrong', it might have been suitable enough; but when it issues its precept, '*Thou shalt not* steal,' it becomes unmeet; and one who is '*not* under the law, but under grace' must close his ears against it, as an intruder and a tyrant!

Of angels this is said to be the highest felicity, that

'they do *his commandments,* hearkening unto the voice of his word' (Ps. 103:20); just as of those from whom the Lord has 'removed transgression as far as the east is from the west,' it is said that 'they remember *his commandments* to do them' (Ps. 103:12,18). But if this theory of the total disjunction of the law from believers be true, then angels must be in bondage, and they also to whom Paul refers as specimens of the blessed men whose transgressions are forgiven by the imputation of 'righteousness without works' (Rom. 4:6). To unforgiven men law is bondage; but is it so to the forgiven? Do pardoned men hate or love it? Do they dread it or delight in it? Do they disobey it or obey it? Do they dismiss it from their thoughts and consciences, or do they make it their 'meditation all the day'? Yet there are men who speak of law as abrogated to a believer, who look with no favour on those who listen to it, but pity them as ill-taught, ill-informed men, who, if in Christ at all, are only Christians of the lowest grade, the least in the kingdom of heaven.

And this is said to be the proper result of a believed gospel! This is called an essential part of higher Christianity and is reckoned indispensable to the right appreciation of a saint's standing before God. The realising of it is a proof of true spirituality and the denial of it an evidence of imperfect knowledge and a cramped theology!

We can find no such spirituality, no such Christianity in the Bible. This is licence, not liberty; it is freedom *to* sin, not freedom *from* sin. It may be spiritual sentimentalism, but it is not spirituality. It is sickly religionism, which, while professing a higher standard than mere law, is departing from that healthy and authentic conformity to the will of God which results from the love and study of his statutes. It is framing a new and human standard, in *supplement*, if not in contradiction, of the old and the divine.[3]

This dislike of the law as a rule of life, and a guide to our knowledge, both of what is right and what is wrong, bodes nothing good. It bears no resemblance to the apostle's delight in the law of God after the inner man, but looks like dread of its purity and searching light. Nay, it looks more like the spirit of antichrist than of Christ; the spirit of him whose characteristic is lawlessness ($\dot{\alpha}\nu o\mu\iota\alpha$, 'without law'), than ever of him who, as the obedient Son, ever did the Father's will, in accordance with the holy law. 'I delight to do thy *will*, O my God: yea, thy *law* is within my heart' (Ps. 40:8). It is granted that 'the law worketh wrath' (Rom. 4:15), and yet that to a believing man legal threats of condemnation have no terror. It is granted that, in the matter of forgiveness and acceptance, law is to him nothing, save as seen fulfilled in his Surety; that law has no claim upon him which should break his peace, or trouble his conscience, or bring him into bondage; that law can only touch him and deal with him in the person of his substitute; that the righteousness in which he stands before God is a 'righteousness without the law' and 'without the deeds of the law'; that the sin which still remains in him does not give the law any hold over him, or any right to enforce its old claims or threats. It is granted that it is in grace alone that he stands, and rejoices in hope of the glory of God, in a condition at all times to take up the challenge, 'Who shall lay anything to the charge of

---

3. 'Not without law to God,' says the apostle; nay, 'under the law to Christ' (1 Cor. 9:21, not $\dot{\alpha}\nu o\mu o\varsigma$, but $\dot{\epsilon}\nu\nu o\mu o\varsigma$); and yet he understood well enough what it is to be 'not under the law, but under grace'.

God's elect?' 'Who is he that condemneth?' But admitting fully all this, we ask, 'What is there in this to disjoin him from the law or exempt him from obedience to it? Are not all these things done to him for the purpose of setting him in a position wherein he may love and keep the blessed law which Jesus kept? And should he not feel and cry, as did the redeemed men of other days, 'Oh that my ways were directed to keep thy *statutes*'? (Ps. 119:5). 'Oh let me not wander from they *commandments*' (Ps. 119:10); 'I have rejoiced in the way of thy *testimonies*' (Ps. 119:14); 'my soul breaketh for the longing that it hath unto thy *judgements*' (Ps. 119:20); 'make me to understand the way of thy *precepts*' (Ps. 119:27); 'I will run in the way of thy *commandments* when thou shalt enlarge my heart' (Ps. 119:32).[4] (See Appendix, Note 12).

Should anyone say that it is not to *service* but to *bondage* they object, I answer, no one contends for bondage. It is in the spirit of adoption and filial love that we obey the law, even as the Son of God obeyed it. But it is somewhat remarkable that the word which the apostle uses, in reference to *his* connection with law, is not that for *priestly* service or ministration, but for *menial offices*: 'that we should *serve* ($\delta o v \lambda \epsilon v \omega$, be a slave) in newness of spirit' (Rom. 7:6); 'with the mind I myself *serve* the law of God' (Rom. 7:25); 'yield your members *servants* to righteousness' (Rom. 6:19); so that, as the strictest conformity to the law was that in which he delighted, so it is that in which he calls on us to delight.

---

4. The 19th and 119th Psalms must be very uncomfortable reading to those who think that a saint has nothing to do with the law. Will it be said that such legal Psalms were only for Old Testament saints!

When he speaks of not being 'under the law' but 'delivered from the law', his meaning is so obvious that it is somewhat difficult to misunderstand him. His whole argument is to show how the law affected a sinner's standing before God, either in condemning or in justifying. He shows that it cannot do the latter but only the former; and that for justification we must go to something else than law; for 'by the deeds of the law shall no flesh be justified'. In everything relating to our justification, everything connected with pardon or the giving of a 'good conscience', we are not under law. But does this release us from conformity to the law? Does this make it less a duty to walk according to its precepts, or make our breaches of law no longer sin? Does our being, in this sense, 'delivered from the law' cancel the necessity of loving God and man? The summing up of the law is, 'Thou shalt love the Lord thy God with all thy heart, and thy neighbour as thyself.' Is a saint not under obligation so to love? Would the fulfilment of this be bondage and inconsistent with the spirit of adoption? Is liberty claimed for a Christian either to love or not to love, as he pleases? If he does not love, is he not sinning? Or does his not being under law, but under grace, make the want of love no crime? Is obedience a matter of option, not of obligation? If it is answered, No; we will love God with all our heart, but not because the law enjoins; I answer this looks very like the spirit of a froward child, who says to a parent, I will do such and such a thing because I please, but not because you bid me.

As the common objections to the observance of the Sabbath take for granted that that day is a curse and not a blessing – bondage, not liberty – so the usual objections to the keeping of the law assume that it is in itself an evil, not a good, an enemy and not a friend.

Say what men will, obedience to law is liberty, compliance with law is harmony, not discord. The *force* of law does not need always to be *felt,* but its object, whether felt or unfelt, is to keep everything in its proper place, and moving in its proper course, so that one man's liberty may not interfere with another man's, but each have the greatest amount of actual freedom which creaturehood is capable of, without harm to itself or others. Law does not interfere with true liberty, but only with that which is untrue, promoting and directing the former, discouraging only the latter.

As with the orbs of heaven, so with us. Obedience to their ordered courses is not simply a necessity of their *being,* but of their *liberty.* Let them snap their cords, and choose for themselves the unfettered range of space; then not only is order gone, and harmony gone, and beauty gone, but *liberty* is gone; for that which keeps them in freedom is obedience to the forces of their constitution, and non-departure from their appointed orbits. Disobedience to these, departure from these, would bring about immediate collision of star with star, the stoppage of their happy motions, the extinction of their joyful light, havoc and death, star heaped on star in universal wreck.

CHAPTER 7

THE SAINT AND THE
SEVENTH OF THE ROMANS

And I will put enmity between thee and the woman, and between thy seed and her seed; it shall bruise thy head, and thou shalt bruise his heel (Gen. 3:15).

Who can understand his errors? cleanse thou me from secret faults. Keep back thy servant also from presumptuous sins; let them not have dominion over me: then shall I be upright, and I shall be innocent from the great transgression (Ps. 19:12, 13).

Iniquities prevail against me: as for our transgressions, thou shalt purge them away (Ps. 65:3).

My soul cleaveth unto the dust: quicken thou me according to thy word (Ps. 119:25).

Then said I, Woe is me! for I am undone; because I am a man of unclean lips, and I dwell in the midst of a people of unclean lips; for mine eyes have seen the King, the LORD of hosts (Isa. 6:5).

For we know that the law is spiritual: but I am carnal, sold under sin. For that which I do, I allow not: for what I would, that do I not; but what I hate, that do I. If then I do that which I would not, I consent unto the law, that it is good. Now then it is no more I that do it, but sin that dwelleth in me. For I know that in me, (that is, in my flesh), dwelleth no good thing; for to will is present with me; but how to perform that which is good I find not. For the good that I would, I do not: but the evil which I would not, that I do. Now if I do that I would not, it is no more I that do it, but sin that dwelleth in me. I find then a law, that, when I would do good, evil is present with me. For I delight in the law of God after the inward man: But I see another law in my members, warring against the law of my mind, and bringing me into captivity to the law of sin which is in my members. O wretched man that I am! who shall deliver me from the body of this death? (Rom. 7:14-24).

For if we would judge ourselves, we should not be judged. But when we are judged, we are chastened of the Lord, that we should not be condemned with the world (1 Cor. 11:31, 32).

For the flesh lusteth against the Spirit, and the Spirit against the flesh: and these are contrary the one to the other: so that ye cannot do the things that ye would (Gal. 5:17).

If we say that we have no sin, we deceive ourselves, and the truth is not in us. If we confess our sins, he is faithful and just to forgive us our sins, and to cleanse us from all unrighteousness. If we say that we have not sinned, we make him a liar, and his word is not in us (1 John 1:8-10).

I do not see how any one, with a right insight into the apostle's argument, without a theory to prop up, or with any personal consciousness of spiritual conflict, could have thought of referring this chapter to a believer's unregenerate condition, or to his transition state, while groping his way to rest.

It furnishes a key to an experience which would otherwise have seemed inexplicable, the solution of perplexities which, without it, would have been a stumbling-block and a mystery. It is God's recognition of the saint's inner conflict as an indispensable process of discipline, as a development of the contrast between light and darkness, as an exhibition of the way in which God is glorified in the infirmities of his saints, and in their contests with the powers of evil. Strike out that chapter, and the existence of sin in a soul after conversion is unexplained. It accounts for the inner warfare of the forgiven man, and gives the apostle's experience as a specimen of the conflict.

The previous chapters in Romans show the man forgiven, justified, dead, and risen with Christ. Is not sin, then, extirpated? The seventh chapter answers, No. It no longer *reigns,* but it *fights.* It does not, indeed, bring back condemnation or bondage or doubt, but it stirs up strife, strife which the completeness of the justification does not hinder, and which the saint's progress in holiness does not arrest, but rather aggravates, so that at times there *seems* to be retrogressions, not advancement in the spiritual life.

'I delight in the law of God after *the inner man,*'[1] are the words, not of an inquirer, or doubter, or semi-regenerate man, but of one who had learned to say, with saints of other days, 'Oh, how love I thy law' (Ps. 119:97); nay, with Messiah himself, 'I delight to do *thy will,* O my God; yea, thy law is *within my heart*' (Ps. 40:8).

'With *the mind* I myself serve the law of God,' is the language of one to whom obedience had become blessedness, and who was not only looking into the perfect law of liberty, but continuing therein (James 1:25), in whose estimation 'serving righteousness' (Rom. 6:18), 'serving God' (Rom. 6:22), 'serving the Lord,' and 'serving the law of God' were equivalents. But then he who thus speaks, this very Paul, who had died and risen with Christ, who had been in the third heaven, adds, 'I see another law in my members, warring against the law of my mind, and bringing me into captivity to the law of sin, which is in my members; O wretched man that I am, who shall deliver me from the body of this death?... So then with the mind I myself serve the law of God, but with the

---

1. χατα τον ἐσω ἀνθρωπον, as in Ephesians 3:16: 'Strengthened with might by his Spirit in the *inner man*'; and in 2 Corinthians 4:16, (where it is ὁ ἐσωθεν), 'the *inner man* is renewed day by day'; showing that this 'inner man' is not perfected at once, but that its renewal is a gradual daily process.

flesh the law of sin.' This is not the language of an unregenerate or half-regenerate man. When, however, he adds, 'I am carnal, sold under sin,' is it really Paul, the new creature in Christ, that he is describing? It is; and they who think it impossible for a saint to speak thus, must know little of sin, and less of themselves. A right apprehension of sin, of one sin or fragment of a sin (if such a thing there be), would produce the oppressive sensation here described by the apostle – a sensation which twenty or thirty years' progress would rather intensify than weaken. They are far mistaken in their estimate of evil who think that it is the *multitude* of sins that gives rise to the bitter outcry, 'I am carnal.' *One sin left behind would produce the feeling here expressed.* But where is the saint whose sins are reduced to one? Who can say, I need the blood less and the Spirit less than I did twenty years ago?

It is to be feared that some are carrying out their idea of 'no condemnation,' of resurrection with Christ, and of the perfection of the new man, to such an extreme as to leave no room for conflict after conversion. They do not see that while conversion calms one kind of storm it raises another, which is to be life-long. To such this seventh of the Romans is as great a vexation as is the ninth to the deniers of divine sovereignty, both being conscious that their theology would be more manageable without the explanations and modifications which these chapters force upon them.

They seem to teach that the regenerate man is made up of two persons, two individuals, the old man and the new man, constituting two separate and independent beings, an angel and a devil linked together – the *old* man unchangeably evil, the *new* perfect and impeccable. (See Appendix, Note 11). In this case one is disposed to ask:

1. Who is responsible for sin committed? Not the new man, for he is 'perfect;' and unless he either sins himself, or helps the old man to sin, he cannot be accountable for the evil done. A good man and a bad one, shut up in one prison, would not agree; but the former, however uncomfortable, would not feel responsible for the sins of the latter. Like David he might mourn that he dwelt in Meshech, or like Lot he might vex his righteous soul with the deeds done around him, but he would not take guilt to himself because of his neighbour's misdeeds. It is the old man *alone,* then, that is the sinner.

2. Who gets the pardon? Is it the old man or the new? Not the new, for he is perfect; and it will hardly be affirmed that it is he who gets pardon for the sins of the old man. It must then be the old man that confesses the sin and gets the forgiveness, and is washed in the blood! Or is there no pardon *needed,* or none *possible,* in such a case? Are the sins of the old man *unpardonable?* If not unpardonable, why is he said to be hopelessly bad?

3. What becomes of the old man at death? Is he cast into hell? Or, if not, what becomes of him? Is he annihilated? If *he* be the sinner, and if his sins are not pardoned, what is to be done with him and with his sins?

4. For whom did Christ die? Not for the *new* man, seeing he is perfect from his creation. It must, then, have been for the *old* man, and for him alone, seeing it is he only that sins!

5. Who is it that dies, is buried, rises, and ascends with Christ? Not the old man, surely? He does not rise again, and sit in heavenly places. Not the new man. He does not die, nor is he buried.

6. Who was it that was born again? Not the *new* man;

he did not need that change. Not the *old* man; he was incapable of it.

7. Who is it that makes progress? Not the old man. He is beyond improvement. Not the new man, for he is perfect. So that there is no room for 'the inner man being renewed day by day'. Scripture teaches that the *whole man* advances, 'increases in the knowledge of God,' the *old* element becoming weaker, and the *new* stronger, and the individual growing in hatred of sin, love to God and Christ, the righteous law, and every holy thing. But how those who insist on the perfection of the new man, and the unchangeableness of the old, can teach progress, we do not see.

These questions, thus asked and answered, lead us to the simple conclusion that the language of the apostle is figurative. 'Not figurative at all,' said a friend to us. 'There is no figure in the matter. Only a rationalist would say so. Bible words are all real and literal.' *Real* I grant; not always *literal.* There are *figures* in Scripture. When the Lord said, 'Beware of the *leaven* of the Pharisees,' he used a figure; and his disciples were wrong in accepting his words *literally. They* were the rationalists. When he said, 'Ye must be *born again,'* he used a figure; and Nicodemus was mistaken in construing his language literally. *He* was the rationalist.

The disciples and Nicodemus, by their literalities, turned our Lord's words into foolishness. So do some among us by their teaching as to the old and new man. If there be no figure, then there must be *two bodies, two souls, two spirits,* those of the old man and the new; for a *man* is a being made up of body, soul, and spirit. If there be no figure here, there will be no figure in Ezekiel 36:26;

and it must be maintained that God literally takes out one heart and puts in another; takes out a stone, and inserts flesh; in which case the old nature disappears entirely, and the new reigns alone.

We know that there is conflict in the soul. But this is not between two persons or personalities, or separate individuals, but between two parts of *one person*. In the case before us, the one person is Paul – once Saul, now Paul. *He* feels himself responsible for the sins of the old man; *he* gets the pardon for the old man's sins; for the old man is but another name for a part of his own very self. It was Paul who was born again, who died and rose with Christ. He was 'begotten again,' not by the insertion of a foreign substance called 'the new creature' into him, but by *his becoming a new creature*. The *whole man* is converted, puts on Christ, is washed in blood, and clothed with the righteousness of God; soul, spirit, conscience, intellect, and will. These are not perfected at once, but the transformation begins at regeneration; and though there are two conflicting elements, there is *one* responsible self or person.

This mysticism as to the old and new man proceeds on a confusion similar to that which mixes up justification and sanctification. The 'old man,' in the apostle's figure, evidently means sometimes our former *legal* condition, and at other times our former *moral* state. In the first sense, the old man is 'crucified,' 'put off,' once for all, in believing, when we cease to have 'confidence in *the flesh*' (Phil. 3:3). *Thus far* it is true that it is not amended, but set aside entirely. In the second sense, there is a daily putting off what is old, and putting on what is new. It is like our putting on Christ, which is done *once for all* at justification,

but also *gradually* in the process of renewing, so that in
one place we read, 'Ye have put on Christ' (Gal. 3:27),
and in another, 'Put ye on the Lord Jesus Christ' (Rom.
13:14). The mixture of these two things is the chief source
of the errors we have been exposing.

This mysticism or confusion is a serious thing. It has
been sometimes taught in such a way, as to lead men to
believe that their peace rested on the perfection or
impeccability of the new man. They were taught that the
new man could not sin; that all sin came from the old man,
whom they had put off; and that, therefore, they did not
need to trouble themselves about sin. No doubt the
consciences of *some* of these misled individuals shrunk
from the full application of this Antinomianism, but *others*
went on in sin, not so much because grace abounded, as
because they were not responsible for the sins indulged
in. The new man in them did not commit the sin, *it was
the old man who did it all;* and what better could be
expected of one who was totally incorrigible!

Thus the foundations were destroyed; the ground of
reconciliation was not the blood of the sin-bearer, but the
new man; the foundation of peace was a *perfect self,* and
not a *perfect Christ.* Nay, Christ was made the minister of
sin, and all manner of evil was justified on the plea that
the new man could not sin.

This doctrine, as sometimes stated, reads not amiss. It
looks plausible, as professing to rest on the very words of
Scripture. But it only needs a slight analysis, a little taking
to pieces, to show that its effect, if carried out, would be
to destroy the feeling of responsibility, to weaken the sense
of sin, to blunt the edge of conscience, to shift the
foundation of a sinner's peace from Christ to self, to render

the blood of sprinkling unnecessary, to hinder personal holiness, and to supersede the work of the Holy Spirit in the soul. For, as to this last, if the doctrine be true, there is no room for the Spirit's operation, any more than for the blood, as he cannot work in the old man and does not need to work in the new.

That the Christian is not responsible for sin committed against his better will, nay, that sin in the Christian is not sin at all, has been maintained from Romans 7:17: 'It is no more I that do it but sin that dwelleth in me.' In this, however, the apostle is not shaking off responsibility from himself, but explaining a fact, giving the solution of a difficulty; and the verse contains one of these peculiar Oriental negatives which the imperfection of human speech renders necessary in order to bring out *the whole* of a great but complex truth, which, in less peculiar language, could not be perfectly enunciated.

The passage is only one out of several, exhibiting the same apparently contradictory form of assertion. The others are as follow: Galatians 2:20: 'I live, *yet not I*, but Christ liveth in me'; 1 Corinthians 7:10: 'Unto the married I command, *yet not I*, but the Lord'; 1 Corinthians 15:10: 'I laboured, *yet not I*, but the grace of God which was with me'; Matthew 10:22: '*It is not ye* that speak, but the Spirit of your Father which speaketh in you'; 2 Corinthians 12:5: 'Of such a one will I glory, *yet of myself I will not* glory.'

From these examples it is plain that the apostle in Romans 7:17 did not intend to disavow either personality or responsibility or free agency, but simply to affirm the existence in himself of an overmastering element or power of evil, the conscious-ness of which led to the statement, 'I am carnal, sold under sin,' and to the exclamation, 'O wretched man that I am, who shall deliver me from the body of this death?'

The dislike which some have to consider this chapter as expository of a saint's daily conflict is by no means a safe sign of their religion or their theology. That peace with God through the blood of Christ should be the beginning of *warfare* seems to us one of the most inevitable conclusions from the gospel, whether of Christ or of Paul; nay, and farther back than this, from the first promise regarding the seed of the woman and the seed of the serpent; and this warfare, internal no less than external, has filled up the life of every saint from the beginning. Apostolical conflict is but a reproduction of patriarchal. Abel and Stephen, Noah and Peter, Abraham and Paul, move over the same battlefield; for the church is one, her covenant one, her warfare one, her victory and glory one. Each saint has 'groaned, being burdened'; the groan has deepened as the light increased, and the New Testament fulness of liberty, instead of diminishing, has intensified the conflict.

One can imagine David or Elijah perplexed about this unending war. How thankful they would have been for the seventh of the Romans, as the clearing up of the mystery! Yet they fought on, as men fight in the twilight or the mist; they finished their course and won their crown. And shall we, in these last days, fling away the key to the mystery which the Holy Spirit has given us by Paul? Or shall we get quit of the mystery by denying the existence of the conflict? Shall we stifle conscience by calling that no sin which is sin? Shall we extenuate trespass because found in a saint? Shall we sit easy under evil, because done by the old man, not the new; by the flesh, and not the spirit? Shall we nurse our spiritual pride by calling the internal conflict an abnormal and unnecessary phase of Christian life, ascribing it to imperfect teaching, or meagre faith, or the retention of the beggarly elements of Jewish bondage?[2]

---

2. We may notice here 1 John 3:9: 'Whosoever is born of God doth not commit sin.' This cannot mean that no man, once born again, ever commits sin; in that case there is no Christian upon earth. The apostle, in 1:7-8, takes for granted that the Christian *does* commit sin; nay, that he dare not say he has no sin without making God a liar, and showing that the truth is not in him. He means to affirm that the being born of God is the only way of deliverance from sin, and that holiness is the true and natural result of being born of God. This kind of affirmation is common. See Romans 14:7: 'None of us liveth to himself, and no man dieth to himself,' that is, such is the life which might be expected from us. Romans 13:4: 'He is the minister of God to thee for good,' that is, he would be, if he fulfilled his office. It is added, 'He *cannot* sin, because he is born of God,' that is, it is totally contrary to his nature to sin. See Matthew 7:18: 'A good tree *cannot* bring forth evil fruit,' that is, it is contrary to its nature to do so, though it sometimes does. Mark 2:19: 'While the bridegroom is with them they *cannot* fast,' that is, it would be incongruous and unnatural. Compare such passages as the following: Luke 11:7, 14:20; John 7:7; 8:43, 9:4, 12:39; Acts 4:16,20; 1 Corinthians 2:14; 10:21; 2 Corinthians 13:8. These passages show that 'cannot' often means, not that the thing does not or might not occur, but that its occurrence is wholly against the nature of things. 'Whoso abideth in him sinneth not' (v. 6), that is, this is the true and only preservation from sin. 'God's seed remaineth in us;' for we are 'born again, not of corruptible *seed*, but of incorruptible, by the word of God' (1 Pet. 1:23).

CHAPTER 8

THE TRUE CREED AND THE TRUE LIFE

And he stretched forth his hand towards his disciples, and said, Behold my mother, and my brethren! For whosoever shall do the will of my Father which is in heaven, the same is my brother, and sister, and mother (Matt. 12:49, 50).

He that hath my commandments, and keepeth them, he it is that loveth me: and he that loveth me shall be loved of my Father, and I will love him, and will manifest myself to him. Judas saith unto him, not Iscariot, Lord, how is it that thou wilt manifest thyself unto us, and not unto the world? Jesus answered and said unto him, If a man love me, he will keep my words: and my Father will love him, and we will come unto him, and make our abode with him (John 14:21-23).

Sanctify them through thy truth: thy word is truth. As thou hast sent me into the world, even so have I also sent them into the world. And for their sakes I sanctify myself, that they also might be sanctified through the truth (John 17:17-19).

I beseech you therefore, brethren, by the mercies of God, that ye present your bodies a living sacrifice, holy, acceptable unto God, which is your reasonable service (Rom. 12:1).

So that ye come behind in no gift; waiting for the coming of our Lord Jesus Christ (1 Cor. 1:7).

Though I speak with the tongues of men and of angels, and have not charity, I am become as sounding brass, or a tinkling cymbal. And though I have the gift of prophecy, and understand all mysteries, and all knowledge; and though I have all faith, so that I could remove mountains, and have not charity, I am nothing. And though I bestow all my goods to feed the poor, and though I give my body to be burned, and have not charity, it profiteth me nothing. Charity suffereth long, and is kind, charity envieth not; charity vaunteth not itself, is not puffed up. Doth not behave itself unseemly, seeketh not her own, is not easily provoked, thinketh no evil; Rejoiceth not in iniquity, but rejoiceth in the truth; Beareth all things, believeth all things, hopeth all things, endureth all things. Charity never faileth; but whether there be prophecies, they shall fail; whether there be tongues, they shall cease; whether there be knowledge, it shall vanish away. For we know in part, and we prophecy in part. But when that which is perfect is come, then that which is in part shall be done away. When I was a child, I spake as a child, I understood as a child, I thought as a child; but when I became a man, I put away childish things. For now we see through a glass, darkly; but then face to face: now I know in part; but then shall I know even as also I am known. And now abideth faith, hope, charity, these three; but the greatest of these is charity (1 Cor. 13:1-13).

Till we all come in the unity of the faith, and of the knowledge of the Son of God, unto a perfect man, unto the measure of the stature of the fulness of Christ: That we henceforth be no more children, tossed to and fro, and carried about with every wind of doctrine, by the sleight of men, and cunning craftiness, whereby they lie in wait to deceive; But speaking the truth in love, may grow up into him in all things, which is the head, even Christ: From whom the whole body fitly joined together, and compacted by that which every joint supplieth, according to the effectual working in the measure of every part, maketh increase of the body unto the edifying of itself in love (Eph. 4:13-16).

That I may know him, and the power of his resurrection, and the fellowship of his sufferings, being made conformable unto his death; If by any means I might attain unto the resurrection of the dead. Not as though I had already attained, either were already perfect: but I follow after, if that I may apprehend that for which also I am apprehended of Christ Jesus. Brethren, I count not myself to have apprehended: but this one thing I do, forgetting those things which are behind, and reaching forth unto those things which are before. I press toward the mark for the prize of the high calling of God in Christ Jesus (Phil. 3:10-14).

Finally, brethren, whatsoever things are true, whatsoever things are honest, whatsoever things are just, whatsoever things are pure, whatsoever things are lovely, whatsoever things are of good report; if there be any virtue, and if there be any praise, think on these things (Phil. 4:8).

THE alphabet of gospel truth is that 'Christ died for our sins' (1 Cor. 15:3). 'By this we are saved,' obtaining peace with God and 'access into THIS GRACE wherein we stand' (Rom. 5:2).

But he who thus believes is also made 'partaker of Christ' (Heb. 3:14); 'partaker of the divine nature' (2 Peter 1:4); 'partaker of the heavenly calling' (Heb. 3:1); 'partaker of the Holy Ghost' (Heb. 3:1); 'partaker of his holiness' (Heb. 12:10). In the person of his Surety he has risen as well as died; he has ascended to the throne, is 'seated with Christ in heavenly places' (Eph. 2:6); his 'life is hid with Christ in God' (Col. 1:3). That which he is to be in the day of the Lord's appearing, he is regarded as being now, and treated by God as such. Faith, in one aspect, bids him look forward to the glory; in another, it bids him look back upon this weary land as if he had already finished his pilgrimage. 'Ye ARE COME to mount Zion, to the city of the living God, to the heavenly Jerusalem' (Heb. 12:22).

Surely, then, a Christian man is called to be consistent and decided, as well as joyful; 'not conformed to *this world*' (Rom. 12:2), but to *that* 'world to come,' in which he already dwells by faith. 'What manner of person ought he to be in all holy conversation and godliness' (2 Peter 3:11).

It has been matter of complaint once and again that some of those who were zealous for these 'higher doctrines,' as they have been called, were not so careful to 'maintain good works,' nor so attentive to the 'minor morals' of Christianity as might have been expected; not so large-hearted, not so open-handed, nor so generous, nor so humble, as many whose light was dimmer; also that they were supercilious; inclined to despise others, as dark and ill-instructed; given to display their consciousness of spiritual superiority in ungentle ways or words.

This will not do. Greater knowledge, lesser love! Higher doctrines, lower morals! Professing to be seated with Christ in heavenly places, yet walking in the flesh, as if proud of their elevation to the right hand of God. Speaking of the perfection of the new man in them, yet exhibiting some of the worst features of the old. Certainly, one who is 'risen with Christ' ought to be like the risen One. He will be expected to be meek and lowly, gentle and loving, simple and frank, kind and obliging, liberal and generous, not easily provoked or affronted, transparent and honest, not selfish, narrow, covetous, conceited, worldly, unwilling to be taught.

Scripture is wonderfully *balanced* in all its parts; let our study of it be the same that we may be *well-balanced* men. The study of prophetic word must not supersede that of the Proverbs, nor must we search the latter merely to discover the traces of the 'higher doctrines' which may be found in that book. We must not overlook the homely, and the little, and the common; we must stoop to the petty moralities, and courtesies, and honesties of tamer life, not neglecting those parts of Scripture which treat of these as vapid or obsolete, but bringing them to bear upon each step of our daily walk, and delighting in them as the wisdom of the God only wise. There is a vitiated *literary* taste, arising not so much from reading what is bad, as from exclusive study of one class of books, and these perhaps the more exciting. There is also a vitiated *spiritual* taste, not necessarily growing out of error or the study of unsound books, but arising from *favouritism* in the reading of Scripture, which shows itself both in the preference of certain parts to others, and in the propensity to search these others only for their references to certain favourite truths. Let the *whole soul* be fed by the study of the *whole Bible,* that so there may be no irregularity nor inequality in the growth of its parts and powers. Let us beware of 'itching' ears and eyes. True, we must not be 'babes,' unable to relish strong meat, and 'unskilful in the word of right-eousness' (Heb. 5:13). But we need to beware of the soarings of an ill-balanced theology and an ill-knit creed. True Christianity is healthy and robust, not soft, nor sickly, nor sentimental; yet, on the other hand, not hard, nor lean, nor ill-favoured, nor ungenial.(See Appendix, Note 13).

'Brethren, be not children in understanding; howbeit, in malice be ye children, but in understanding BE MEN' (1 Cor. 14:20).

We want not merely a high and full theology, but we want that theology *acted out* in life, embodied nobly in daily doings, without anything of what the world calls 'cant' or 'simper'. The higher the theology, the higher and the manlier should be the life resulting from it. It should give to the Christian character and bearing a divine erectness and simplicity; true dignity of demeanour, without pride, or stiffness, or coldness; true strength of will, without obstinacy, or caprice, or waywardness. The higher the doctrine is, the more ought it to bring us into contact with the *mind* of God which is 'the truth,' and with the *will* of God which is 'the law'. He who concludes that, because he has reached the region of the 'higher doctrines,' he may soar above the law, or above creeds, or above churches, or above the petty details of common duty, would need to be on his guard against a blunted conscience, a self-made religion, and a wayward life.

Though 'set on high,' we 'regard the things that are lowly;' we prize the lofty teaching of the epistles, but we prize no less 'the law and the prophets'. We listen to the apostolic doctrine, and learn to say, 'I am crucified with Christ, nevertheless I live; yet not I, but Christ liveth in me' (Gal. 2:20); yet we do not turn away from the apostolic *precepts*, as beneath us: 'put away lying;' 'speak every man truth with his neighbour;' 'let him that stole steal no more;' 'let all bitterness, and wrath and anger, and clamour, and evil-speaking be put away from you with all malice;' 'uncleanness and covetousness let it not be once named among you, neither filthiness, nor foolish talking, nor jesting;' 'put off all these, anger, wrath, malice, blasphemy, filthy communication;' 'lie not one to another, seeing ye have put off the old man with his deeds.'

If it seem strange to some, to be told that a redeemed and risen man must be a doer of the law, does it not seem still more strange that one entrusted with the ministry should have such minute precepts as these enjoined, 'not given to wine, no striker, not greedy of filthy lucre, not a brawler, not covetous.' These are the *commandments* of the Holy Ghost, and they are LAW just as truly as that which was proclaimed in Horeb amid the fire and darkness. And the true question with us (as we have seen) is not whether we are to obey this law or that law, but *any law at all*. If obedience to apostolic law be not legalism, then neither is obedience to the moral law; and if our oneness with Christ exempts or disjoins us from the moral law, it exempts and disjoins us from *all law whatsoever*, for everything in the shape of law, or precept, or command- ment, contained in Scripture, is from the one Spirit of God, whether in the Book of Exodus or the Epistle to the

Romans. We know, indeed, that what is merely ritual or ceremonial is gone, being exhausted and put away by Christ; but what is moral and spiritual remains, and must remain for ever; not one jot or tittle of it can fail. What was moral or immoral four thousand years ago is the same still. What was moral or immoral to the Jew is so to the Gentile still. An Old Testament and a New Testament saint rest on the same rock, are washed in the same blood, eat the same spiritual meat, and drink the same spiritual drink (1 Cor. 10:3), have put on the same Christ, are doers of the same law, are members of the same body, are heirs of the same crown (Matt. 8:11; 21:43; Luke 13:28; Rom. 11:18; Heb. 11:40; Rev. 7:9-15).

'The law is good if a man use it lawfully,' says the apostle, but according to some, the only lawful way of using it is *not to use it at all*.[1] (See Appendix, Note 12).

The higher life, then, is not a life against law, nor a life without law, nor a life above law, but a life like that of the great Law-fulfiller, a life in which the law finds its fullest and most perfect development. It was so in Jesus; it is so in us in so far as we resemble him in spirit and walk. It is a thoroughly conscientious, upright, honourable life. Some,

---

1. True, 'the law is not made for the righteous man,' but for 'unholy and profane, for murderers and manslayers' (1 Tim. 1:9); and as a traveller who keeps the middle of the way never comes into collision with the fences on either side, so a quiet citizen has no need to concern himself about the laws against murder. Man's law does not touch him who keeps it, but him who breaks it; yet it speaks to every one, it is a guide to every one, and the principles or moralities of law are wrought into every one, and wrought the most into those for whom it was 'not made'; so that they who never come into collision with it are just those who are unconsciously, yet thoroughly obeying it.

indeed, seem to identify conscientiousness with bondage; but between the two there is no resemblance, save when the conscience is unenlightened, or has become diseased and weak. When the nervous system of the body falls into disorder, then often does Satan (through this inlet) enter the soul, and perplex the conscience; magnifying fancied sin, and palliating real sin; making men mistake a *diseased* for a *tender* conscience. But this ought not to lead to the disparagement of thorough conscientiousness in one who has died and risen with Christ; conscientiousness in little things as well as great, in business, in the ordering of our households, in the laying out of our time and our money, in fulfilling engagements, in keeping promises, in discharging duties, in bearing witness for Christ, in nonconformity to the world.

The man who knows that he is risen with Christ, and has set his affection on things above, will be a just, trusty, ingenuous, unselfish, truthful man. He will 'add to his faith virtue, and to virtue knowledge, and to knowledge temperance, and to temperance patience, and to patience godliness, and to godliness brotherly kindness, and to brotherly kindness charity' (2 Pet. 1:5-7). He will seek not to be 'barren nor unfruitful'. 'Whatsoever things are true, whatsoever things are honest, whatsoever things are just, whatsoever things are pure, whatsoever things are lovely, whatsoever things are of good report,' these he will think upon and do.

For there is some danger of falling into a soft and effeminate Christianity, under the plea of a lofty and ethereal theology. Christianity was born for endurance; not an exotic, but a hardy plant, braced by the keen wind; not languid, nor childish, nor cowardly. It walks with firm step and erect frame; it is kindly, but firm; it is gentle, but honest; it is calm, but not facile; obliging, but not imbecile; decided, but not churlish. It does not fear to speak the stern word of condemnation against error, nor to raise its voice against surrounding evils, under the pretext that it is not of this world; it does not shrink from giving honest reproof, lest it come under the charge of displaying an unchristian spirit. It calls sin *sin,* on whomsoever it is found, and would rather risk the accusation of being actuated by a bad spirit than not discharge an explicit duty. Let us not misjudge strong words used in honest controversy. Out of the heat a viper may come forth; but we shake it off and feel no harm. The religion of both Old and New Testaments is marked by fervent outspoken testimonies against evil. To speak smooth things in such a case may be sentimentalism, but it is not Christianity. It is a betrayal of the cause of truth and righteousness. If any one should be frank, manly, honest, cheerful (I do not say blunt or rude, for a Christian must be courteous and polite), it is he who has tasted that the Lord is gracious, and is looking for and hasting unto the coming of the day of God.

I know that charity covereth a multitude of sins; but it does not call evil good because a good man has done it; it does not excuse inconsistencies because the inconsistent brother has a high name and a fervent spirit; crookedness and worldliness are still crookedness and worldliness, though exhibited in one who seems to have reached no common height of attainment.

I know also that in this world we shall be evil spoken of, and that it is hopeless to attempt to answer every charge. But let us not suffer an accusation to lie upon us, under the pretext that God will take care of our good name, when

perhaps the secret reason was that there was some
foundation for the evil report against us, and that our good
name had better not be brought to a too public test. Let us
clear ourselves when the opportunity presents or the
occasion demands. It is not wrong to be jealous of our
good name, and to answer frankly the fair questionings of
friend or foe. It will be time enough to suffer martyrdom
when we are actually tied to the stake. It is foolish and
feeble to try to become martyrs before the time. Paul met
accusations bravely and would not allow his good to be
evil spoken of (Acts 28:17; 2 Cor. 8:20-21; 11:9; 12:18-
19). Our reformers met their slanderers bravely, and though
they could not stay the pen of the defamer, yet furnished
materials for vindicating themselves and their cause, most
amply. There was only ONE who was dumb as a sheep
before her shearers, who answered not a word; and he was
silent because the chastisement of our peace was upon
him, and to be made of 'no reputation' was one part of the
penalty he was enduring.

Yet let us know when to be silent, as well as when to
speak. It is not always right or seemly to answer a fool
according to his folly. Let us learn to bear and to forbear;
'giving no offence in anything,' nor letting 'our good be
evil spoken of;' seeking the things which make for peace,
and the things whereby we may edify one another;
'providing for honest things (2 Cor. 8:21: *kala*, things
excellent or beautiful), not only in the sight of God, *but
also in the sight of men*'; having 'a conscience void of
offence toward God and toward men' (Acts 24:16,20).
These are memorable words, 'The kingdom of God is not
meat and drink; but righteousness, and peace, and joy in
the Holy Ghost. For he that in these things serveth Christ

is ACCEPTABLE TO GOD, AND APPROVED OF MEN' (Rom. 14:17,18).

With many of us the Christian life has not gone on to maturity. 'Ye did run well, who did hinder you?' It has been a work well begun but left unfinished; a battle boldly entered on but only half fought out; a book with but the preface written, no more. Is not thus Christ dishonoured? Is not his gospel thus misrepresented, his cross denied, his words slighted, his example set at nought? Are sunsets such as we have too often witnessed, the true endings of the bright dawns which we have welcomed? *Must* suns go down at noon? *Must* Ephesus leave her first love, Laodicea grow lukewarm, and Sardis cold? Are issues such as these inevitable and universal? Or shall we not protest against them as failures, perversions, crimes – altogether inexcusable?

Did a holy life consist of one or two noble deeds, some signal specimens of doing or enduring or suffering, we might account for the failure and reckon it small dishonour to turn back in such a conflict. But a holy life is made up of a multitude of small things. It is the little things of the hour, and not the great things of the age, that fill up a life like that of Paul and John, like that of Rutherford or Brainerd or Martyn. Little words, not eloquent speeches or sermons; little deeds, not miracles, nor battles, nor one great heroic act or mighty martyrdom; make up the true Christian life. The little constant sunbeam, not the lightning; the waters of Siloah 'that go softly' in their meek mission of refreshment, not 'the waters of the river great and many,' rushing down in torrent-noise and force; are the true symbols of a holy life.

The avoidance of little evils, little sins, little

inconsistencies, little weaknesses, little follies, little indiscretions and imprudencies, little foibles, little indulgences of self and of the flesh, little acts of indolence or indecision or slovenliness or cowardice, little equivocations or aberrations from high integrity, little touches of shabbiness and meanness, little bits of covetousness and penuriousness, little exhibitions of worldliness and gaiety, little indifferences to the feelings or wishes of others, little outbreaks of temper or crossness or selfishness or vanity – the avoidance of such *little* things as these goes far to make up at least the negative beauty of a holy life.

And then attention to the little duties of the day and hour, in public transactions or private dealings or family arrangements; to little words and looks and tones; little benevolences or forbearances or tendernesses; little self-denials and self-restraints and self-forgetfulnesses; little plans of quiet kindness and thoughtful consideration for others; to punctuality and method and true aim in the ordering of each day – these are the active developments of a holy life, the rich and divine mosaics of which it is composed. What makes yon green hill so beautiful? Not the outstanding peak or stately elm, but the bright sward which clothes its slopes, composed of innumerable blades of slender grass. It is of small things that a great life is made up; and he who will acknowledge no life as great save that which is built up of great things, will find little in Bible characters to admire or copy.

If we would aim at a holy and useful life, let us learn to redeem time. 'I am large about redeeming time,' says Richard Baxter in the *Preface to his Christian Directory*, 'because therein the sum of a holy obedient life is

included.' Yes; 'let us redeem the time because the days
are evil' (Eph. 5:16; Col. 4:5). A wasted life is the result
of unredeemed time. Desultory working, impulsive giving,
fitful planning, irregular reading, ill-assorted hours,
perfunctory or unpunctual execution of business, hurry
and bustle, loitering and unreadiness – these, and such
like, are the things which take out the whole pith and power
from life, which hinder holiness, and which eat like a
canker into our moral being, which make success and
progress an impossibility, either as regards ourselves or
others. There needs not to be routine, but there must be
regularity; there ought not to be mechanical stiffness, but
there must be order; there may not be haste, but there must
be no trifling with our own time or that of others;
'Whatsoever thy hand findeth to do, do it with thy might'
(Eccles. 9:10). If the thing is worth doing at all, it is worth
doing well; and, in little things as well as great, we must
show that we are in earnest. There must be no idling, but a
girding up of the loins; a running the race with patience;
the warring of a good warfare; steadfastness and perseverance, 'always abounding in the work of the Lord.' The
flowers are constant in their growing, the stars are constant
in their courses, the rivers are constant in their flowing;
they lose no time; so must our life be, not one of fits or
starts or random impulses; not one of levity or inconstancy
or fickle scheming, but steady and resolute; the life of men
who know their earthly mission and have their eye upon
the heavenly goal.

A holy life in man's estimation may be simply a life of
benevolence, or of austerity, or of punctual devotion, or
of kindly geniality, or noble uprightness, or liberal
sympathy with all creeds, all sects, all truths, and all errors.

But a holy life in God's estimation, and according to Bible teaching, must be founded upon *truth,* must begin personally in conscious peace with God through the blood of the everlasting covenant; must grow with the increase of truth and deliverance from error; must be maintained by fellowship with God, in Christ Jesus, through the indwelling of the 'Spirit of holiness'. Error or imperfect truth must hinder holiness. Uncertainty as to our reconciliation with God must cloud us, straiten us, fetter us, and so prevent the true holiness, besides also fostering the false. Fellowship must be reserved unbroken, that the transmission of the heavenly electricity, in all its sanctifying, quickening power, may go on uninterrupted. Nothing must come between; not the world, nor self, nor the flesh, nor vanity, nor idols, nor the love of ease and pleasure.

The word must be studied in all its fulness. Over its whole length and breadth we must spread ourselves. Above all theologies and creeds and catechisms and books and hymns must the word be meditated on, that we may grow in the knowledge of all its parts, and in assimilation to its models. Our souls must be steeped in it; not in certain favourite parts of it, but in the whole. We must know it, not from the report of others, but from our own experience and vision, else will our life be but an imitation, our religion second-hand, and therefore second-rate. Another cannot breathe the air for us, nor eat for us, nor drink for us. We must do these for ourselves. So no one can do our religion for us, nor infuse into us the life or truth which he may possess. These are not things of proxy or merchandise, or human impartation. Out of the book of God and by the Spirit of God must each one of us be taught, else we learn in vain. Hence the exceeding danger of human influence or authority. A place of influence in such a case becomes perilous alike to the possessor of the influence and to those over whom that sway is wielded. Even when altogether on the side of truth, its issue may be but an unfruitful formalism, a correct petrifaction, an intelligent orthodoxy, and both they who possess the influence or are under its power ought to be greatly on their guard lest the human supplant the divine, and 'the fear of God be taught by the precept of men' (Isa. 29:13); lest an artificial piety be the result, a mere facsimile religion, without vitality, without comfort, and without influence.

One who has 'learned of Christ,' who 'walks with God,' will not be an *artificial* man; not one playing a part or sustaining a character. He will be thoroughly *natural* in manners, words, looks, tones and habits. He will be like that most natural of all creatures, a little child. Christianity becomes repulsive the moment that it is suspected to be fictitious. Religion must be ingenuous. No affectation, nor pedantry, nor conceit, nor set airs, nor what the world calls 'whining,' can serve the cause of Christ, or give weight to character, or win an adversary of the cross. The 'epistles of Christ,' to be 'known and read of all men,' must be transparent and natural. In living for Christ, we must follow HIM fully, not copying a copy, but copying HIMSELF; otherwise ours will be an imperfect testimony, a reflected and feeble religion, devoid of ease, and simplicity, and grace; bearing the marks of imitation and art, if not of forgery.

CHAPTER 9

COUNSELS AND WARNINGS

LORD, who shall abide in thy tabernacle? who shall dwell in thy holy hill? He that walketh uprightly, and worketh righteousness, and speaketh the truth in his heart. He that backbiteth not with his tongue, nor doeth evil to his neighbour, nor taketh up a reproach against his neighbour. In whose eyes a vile person is contemned; but he honoureth them that fear the LORD. He that sweareth to his own hurt, and changeth not. He that putteth not out his money to usury, nor taketh reward against the innocent. He that doeth these things shall never be moved (Ps. 15:1-5).

My son, if thou wilt receive my words, and hide my commandments with thee; So that thou incline thine ear unto wisdom, and apply thine heart to understanding; Yea, if thou criest after knowledge, and liftest up thy voice for understanding; If thou seekest her as silver, and searchest for her as for hid treasures; Then shalt thou understand the fear of the LORD, and find the knowledge of God. For the LORD giveth wisdom: out of his mouth cometh knowledge and understanding. He layeth up sound wisdom for the righteous: he is a buckler to them that walk uprightly. He keepeth the paths of judgment, and preserveth the way of his saints. Then shalt thou understand righteousness, and judgment, and equity; yea, every good path (Prov. 2:1-9).

My covenant was with him of life and peace; and I gave them to him for the fear wherewith he feared me, and was afraid before my name. The law of truth was in his mouth, and iniquity was not found in his lips: he walked with me in peace and equity, and did turn many away from iniquity (Mal. 2:5, 6).

Be ye therefore perfect, even as your Father which is in heaven is perfect (Matt. 5:48).

I beseech you therefore, brethren, by the mercies of God, that ye present your bodies a living sacrifice, holy, acceptable unto God, which is your reasonable service. And be not conformed to this world: but be ye transformed by the renewing of your mind, that ye may prove what is that good, and acceptable, and perfect, will of God. For I say, through the grace given unto me, to every man that is among you, not to think of himself more highly than he ought to think; but to think soberly, according as God hath dealt to every man the measure of faith. For as we have many members in one body, and all members have not the same office; So we, being many, are one body in Christ, and every one members one of another. Having then gifts differing according to the grace that is given to us, whether prophecy, let us prophesy according to the proportion of faith; Or ministry, let us wait on our ministering; or he that teacheth, on teaching; Or he that exhorteth, on exhortation: he that giveth, let him do it with simplicity; he that ruleth, with diligence; he that sheweth mercy, with cheerfulness. Let love be without dissimulation. Abhor that which is evil; cleave to that which is good. Be kindly affectioned one to another with brotherly love; in honour preferring one another; not slothful in business; fervent in spirit; serving the Lord; Rejoicing in hope; patient in tribulation; continuing instant in prayer; Distributing to the necessity of saints; given to hospitality. Bless them which persecute you: bless, and curse not. Rejoice with them that do rejoice, and weep with them that weep. Be of the same mind one toward another. Mind not high things, but condescend to men of low estate. Be not wise in your own conceits. Recompense to no man evil for evil. Provide things honest in the sight of all men. If it be possible, as much as lieth in you, live peaceably with all men (Rom. 12:1-18).

Finally, my brethren, be strong in the Lord, and in the power of his might. Put on the whole armour of God, that ye may be able to stand against the wiles of the devil. For we wrestle not against flesh and blood, but against principalities, against powers, against the rulers of the darkness of this world, against spiritual wickedness in high places. Wherefore take unto you the whole armour of God, that ye may be able to withstand in the evil day, and having done all, to stand. Stand therefore, having your loins girt about with truth, and having on the breastplate of the gospel of peace; Above all, taking the shield of faith, wherewith ye shall be able to quench all the fiery darts of the wicked. And take the helmet of salvation, and the sword of the Spirit, which is the word of God: Praying always with all prayer and supplication in the Spirit, and watching thereunto with all perseverance and supplication for all saints (Eph. 6:10-18).

If ye then be risen with Christ, seek those things which are above, where Christ sitteth on the right hand of God. Set your affection on things above, not on things on the earth. For ye are dead, and your life is hid with Christ in God. When Christ who is our life, shall appear, then shall ye also appear with him in glory. Mortify therefore your members which are upon the earth; fornication, uncleanness, inordinate affection, evil concupiscence, and covetousness, which is idolatry: For which things' sake the wrath of God cometh on the children of disobedience: In the which ye also walked some time, when ye lived in them. But now ye also put off all these; anger, wrath, malice, blasphemy, filthy communication out of your mouth. Lie not one to another, seeing that ye have put off the old man with his deeds; And have put on the new man, which is renewed in knowledge after the image of him that created him: Where there is neither Greek nor Jew, circumcision nor uncircumcision, Barbarian, Scythian, bond nor free: but Christ is all, and in all. Put on therefore, as the elect of God, holy and beloved, bowels of mercies, kindness, humbleness of mind, meekness, longsuffering; Forbearing one another, and forgiving one another, if any man have a quarrel against any: even as Christ forgave you, so also do ye. And above all these things put on charity, which is the bond of perfectness. And let the peace of God rule in your hearts, to the which also ye are called in one body; and be ye thankful. Let the word of Christ dwell in you richly in all wisdom; teaching and admonishing one another in psalms and hymns and spiritual songs, singing with grace in your hearts to the Lord. And whatsoever ye do in word or deed, do all in the name of the Lord Jesus, giving thanks to God and the Father by him (Col. 3:1-17).

But, beloved, remember ye the words which were spoken before of the apostles of our Lord Jesus Christ; How that they told you there should be mockers in the last time, who should walk after their own ungodly lusts. These be they who separate themselves, sensual, having not the Spirit. But ye, beloved, building up yourselves on your most holy faith, praying in the Holy Ghost. Keep yourselves in the love of God, looking for the mercy of our Lord Jesus Christ unto eternal life. And of some have compassion, making a difference: And others save with fear, pulling them out of the fire; hating even the garment spotted by the flesh. Now unto him that is able to keep you from falling, and to present you faultless before the presence of his glory with exceeding joy, To the only wise God our Saviour, be glory and majesty, dominion and power, both now and ever. Amen (Jude 17-25).

I know thy works, and charity, and service, and faith, and thy patience, and thy works; and the last to be more than the first (Rev. 2:19).

That which, among men, so frequently takes the name of holiness is very unlike the Bible reality. Whether used in connection with the hardness of an unliving orthodoxy, or the genialities of a fond idealism, or the smooth regularities of a mechanical devotion, or the religiousness of pictorial superstition, or the austerities of self-righteous mortification, or the sentimentalisms of liberalized theology, or the warm dreams of an earnest pantheism, the words 'holy' and 'holiness' and 'spirituality' have become misnomers or ciphers, as ambiguous in meaning and profane in use, as would have been Aaron's ephod upon the shoulders of a priest of Baal. This retention of Bible formulas and a Bible terminology after the expulsion or perversion of Bible meaning, is one of the sacrilegious dishonesties of the age, which are so uncomfortably offensive to a straightforward student of the word. (See Appendix, Note 14).

Holiness may be called *spiritual* perfection, as righteousness is *legal* completeness; and both are exhibited in Christ. He is the representation, the illustration, the model. Likeness to him is holiness. He that is holy is conformed to his image. Every other ideal is vanity. We must learn from the four Gospels what *living* holiness is; and for a *doctrinal* exposition of it we must turn to the Epistles. Thus we shall understand both what it is not and what it is.

'Abide in ME,' 'learn of ME,' 'follow ME,' are the contents and summing-up of the Christian statute-book, constituting our true directory and guide in the pursuit of holiness. Here we have:

The Life. From the Prince of Life the new life comes to us; even out of his death and tomb; for 'we are planted together in the likeness of his death that we may be also in that of his resurrection' (Rom. 6:5); 'we are dead (have died), and our life is hid with Christ in God' (Col. 3:3). Thus we are 'alive unto righteousness;' we live, and yet not we, but Christ in us. We come to him for life, or rather, first of all, he comes to us with life; we 'apprehend him', or rather, first of all, 'are apprehended of him'; and the 'abiding in him' is but a continuance of the first act of 'coming;' a doing the same thing all our life which we did at first. Thus we live. Thus life increases by a daily influx; and as yesterday's sunshine will not do for today, nor today's for tomorrow, so must there be the constant communication of heavenly life, else there will be immediate relapse into death and darkness. Because he liveth, we live, and shall live for ever. His life is ours, and our Christianity must be (like its fountainhead) a thing of vitality and power and joy; our life the most genial, earnest and useful of all lives; 'OUT OF US flowing rivers of living water' (John 7:38).

The Scholarship. 'Learn of ME.' His is the school of heaven, the school of light. Here there is all truth and no error. The Tutor is as perfect as he is 'meek and lowly'. He is at once the teacher and the lesson. With him is the perfection of training and discipline and wisdom. There is no flaw, no failure, no incompleteness in the education which he imparts. He teaches to know, to love, to act, to endure, to rejoice, and to be sorrowful, 'to be full and to suffer want.' The range of scholarship enjoyed by his disciples is only to be measured by his divine stores, his 'treasures of wisdom and knowledge'. And the end of his instruction and discipline is to make us holy men, conformed to his likeness, and imitators of his heavenly perfection.

The Walk. 'Follow ME.' It is not a *life* merely to which we are called, but a *walk* (a 'walking about,' as the Greek implies); not a sitting alone; not a private enjoying of religion, but a *walk*; a walk in which we are visible on all sides; a walk which fixes many eyes upon us; a walk in which we are 'made a spectacle' to heaven and earth and hell. It is no motionless resting or retirement from our fellows, but a moving about in the midst of them, a coming into contact with friends and foes, a going to and fro upon the highways and byways of earth. As was the Master so must the servant be. On his way to the cross he looked round and said, 'Follow me' (John 12:26); on his way to the throne, after he had passed the cross, he said the same (John 21:22). To the cross, then, and to the crown alike, we are to follow him. It is one way to both.

He then that would be holy must be like Christ; and he that would be like Christ must be 'filled with the Spirit'; he that would have in him the mind of Christ must have the same 'anointing' as he had, the same indwelling and inworking Spirit; the Spirit of 'adoption', of life, faith, truth, liberty, strength, and holy joy. It is through this mighty quickener that we are quickened; it is through 'sanctification of the Spirit' that we are sanctified (2 Thess. 2:13; 1 Peter 1:2). It is as our *guest* that he does his work; not working without dwelling, nor dwelling without working (2 Tim. 1:14); not exerting a mere influence, like that of music on the ruffled soul, but coming into us and abiding with us; so that being 'filled with his company' as well as pervaded by his power, we are thoroughly 'transformed'; not merely plying us with arguments, nor affecting us with 'moral suasion', but impressing us with the irresistible touch of his divine hand, and penetrating us with his own vital energy, nay, impregnating us with his own purity and life, in spite of desperate resistance and unteachableness and unbelief on our part, all the days of our life.

He that would be like Christ, moreover, must *study* him. We cannot make ourselves holy by merely *trying* to be so, any more than we can make ourselves believe and love by simple energy of endeavour. No force can effect this. Men *try* to be holy, and they fail. They cannot by direct effort work themselves in to holiness. They must gaze upon a holy object; and so be changed into its likeness 'from glory to glory' (2 Cor. 3:18). They must have a holy being for their bosom friend. Companionship with Jesus, like that of John, can alone make us to resemble either the disciple or the Master.

He that would be holy must steep himself in the word, must bask in the sunshine which radiates from each page of revelation. It is through THE TRUTH that we are sanctified (John 17:17). Exposing our souls constantly to this light, we become more thoroughly 'children of the light', and,

> Like the stain'd web that whitens in the sun,
> Grow pure by being purely shone upon.

For, against evil, divine truth is quick and powerful. It acts like some chemical ingredient that precipitates all impurities and leaves the water clear. It works like a spell of disenchantment against the evil one, casting him out, and casting him down. It is 'the sword of the Spirit', with whose keen edge we cut our way through hostile thousands. It is the rod of Moses by which we divide the Red Sea and defeat Amalek and bring water from the desert rock. What evil, what enemy, within or without, is there that can withstand this unconquered and unconquerable word? Satan's object at present is to undermine that word and to disparage its perfection. Let us the more magnify it and the more make constant use of it. It is indeed only a fragment of man's language, made up of human letters and syllables; but it is furnished with superhuman virtue. That rod in the hand of Moses, what was it? A piece of common wood. Yet it cut the Red Sea in twain. That serpent on the pole, what was it? A bit of brass. Yet it healed thousands. Why all this? Because that wood and that brass were connected with Omnipotence, conductors of the heavenly electricity. So let the Bible be to us the book of all books, for wounding, healing, quickening, strengthening, comforting, and purifying.

Yet, he that would be holy must *fight*. He must 'war a good warfare' (1 Tim. 1:18); 'fight the good fight of faith' (1 Tim. 6:12), though not with 'carnal weapons' (2 Cor. 10:4). He must fight upon his knees, 'being sober, and watching unto prayer' (1 Pet. 4:7). He must *wrestle* with principalities and powers, being strong in the Lord and the power of his might, having put on the whole armour of God, girdle, breastplate, shield, helmet, and sword (Eph. 6:12-17). This 'battle is not to the strong' (Eccles. 9:11), but to the weak; it is fought in weakness, and the victory is to them that have 'no might;' for in this conflict 'time and chance' do *not* happen to all; but we count upon victory from the first onset, being made more than conquerors through him that loved us, and are cheered with the anticipation of the sevenfold reward 'to him that overcometh' (Rev. 2:7, etc.). And though, in this our earthly course and combat, we have the hostility of devils, we have the ministry of angels in aid (Heb. 1:14); as well as the power of the Holy Ghost (Eph. 1:13).

He that would be holy must *watch.* 'Watch thou in all things' (2 Tim. 4:5); 'watch ye, stand fast in the faith, quit you like men, be strong' (1 Cor. 14:13). Let the sons of night sleep or stumble in the darkness, but let us, who are of the day, be sober, lest temptation overtake us, and we be ensnared in the wiles of the devil, or the deductions of this wanton world. 'Blessed is he that watcheth' (Rev. 16:15). In watching, too, let us 'witness a good confession' (1 Tim. 6:13), not ashamed of him whose badge we bear; let us run a swift and patient race; 'laying aside every weight, and THE SIN (unbelief) which doth so easily beset us' (Heb. 12:1); 'following after righteousness, godliness, faith, love, patience, meekness' (1 Tim. 6:11), and having our eye upon the coming and the kingdom of our Lord Jesus.

He that would be holy must feel his responsibility for being so, both as a member of Christ's body and a partaker of the Holy Ghost. The thought that perfection is not to be reached here ought not to weaken that sense of responsibility, nor to lead us to give way to aught that would 'grieve the Holy Spirit of God whereby we are sealed unto the day of redemption'. The sevenfold fulness of the risen Christ (Rev. 2:1), and the sevenfold fulness of the Holy Ghost (Rev. 5. 6), these are the church's birthright; and for no mess of pottage is she to sell it; nay, for the personal possession of that fulness, in so far as vessels such as ours can contain it, each saint is responsible.

We are *sanctified by the blood* (Heb. 13:12), that we may
be *sanctified by the Holy Ghost* (1 Cor. 6:11), be 'led by
the Spirit' (Gal. 5:18), be 'temples of the Holy Ghost,'
even in our 'bodies' (1 Cor. 6:19), 'walking' in the Spirit
(Gal. 5:16), 'speaking' by the Spirit (1 Cor. 12:3); 'living'
in the Spirit (Gal. 5:25), and having the 'communion of
the Holy Ghost' (2 Cor. 13:14).[1] (See Appendix, Note 15).

The Christian man must not trifle with sin under any
pretence; least of all on the plea that he is not 'under the
law'. The apostolic precepts and warnings are quite as
explicit as the Mosaic, and much more numerous. He that
thinks himself free from the latter will have no difficulty
in persuading himself that he may set aside the former;
and he who reckons it bondage to listen to the Sinaitic
statute, 'Thou shalt not kill,' will think it equal bondage
to hearken to the Pauline commandments, 'Be not drunk
with wine,' or 'Owe no man anything,' or 'Let him that
stole steal no more.'

As possessors of the Spirit of love, we must be loving,
laying aside all malice and guile and hypocrisies and evil-

---

1. The doctrine of the personality and energy of the Holy Spirit was
not more offensive to the cold infidelity of last century than it is to
the mere earnest and plausible idealism of the present day. It is set
aside as savouring of superstition, and at variance with human liberty
and self-power. Energies from beneath or from above are either denied,
or recognised only as 'principles' or 'sensations,' or developments
of natural law, not connected with personalities in either case.
Supernatural personalities are exploded relics of superstition! The
thought that there was one perfect and superhuman book, in this world
of imperfect literature, used to be cheering; but, if modern theories of
inspiration be true, this consolation is gone, and the world is left
thoroughly disconsolate, without one fragment of the superhuman or
the perfect in the midst of it.

speaking; discharging daily the one debt that is never to be paid (Rom. 13:8). For the indwelling Spirit is not idle nor barren, but produces fruit, divine fruit in human hearts, heavenly fruit on earthly soil, fruit which indicates its inner source, and tells of the glorious guest within; for the fruit of the Spirit is love, joy, peace, long-suffering, gentleness, goodness, faith, meekness, temperance: against such there is no law (Gal. 5. 22-23).

As those whose feet have found the rock, let us be stable, not carried about with every wind of doctrine; not vacillating nor undecided nor compromising. As those who have been 'delivered from a present evil world', let us, like the saints of old, be separate from it, standing aloof from its gaieties, as men who have no time for such things, even were they harmless; keeping our raiment undefiled. Let us be suspicious of its foolish talking and jesting, jealous of its light literature, which 'eats as doth a canker', vitiating the taste, and enervating the soul. Let us maintain unblunted the edge of our relish for prayer and fellowship with God, as the great preservative against the seductions of the age; for only intimacy with God can keep us from intimacy with the world. Let us not try to combine the novel and the Bible, the closet and the ballroom; nor attempt to serve two masters, to drink two cups (1 Cor. 10:21), to worship two gods, to enjoy two religions, to kneel at two altars.

Let us be on our guard against *old self* in every form, whether it be indolence, or temper, or coldness, or rudeness, or disobligingness, or slovenliness, or shabbiness, or covetousness, or flippancy, or self-conceit, or pride, or cunning, or obstinacy, or sourness, or levity, or foolishness, or love of pre-eminence. Let us cultivate a tender conscience, avoiding crotchets and conceits; yet watching against the commission of little sins and the omission of little duties; redeeming the time, yet never in a hurry; calm, cheerful, frank, happy, genial, generous, disinterested, thoughtful of others; and seeing we must protest against the world on so many important points, let us try to differ from it as little as possible on things indifferent, always showing love to those we meet with, however irreligious and unlovable, especially avoiding a contemptuous spirit or an air of superiority.

As disciples of Christ, let our discipleship be complete and consistent; our connection with him exhibiting itself in conformity to his likeness; our life a comprehensive creed; our walk the embodiment of all that is honest and lovely and of good report. Christ's truth sanctifies as well as liberates; his wisdom purifies as well as quickens; let us beware of accepting the liberty without the holiness, the wisdom without the purity, the peace without the zeal and love.

Let us be *true* men, in the best sense of the word; true to ourselves; true to our new birth and our new name; true to the church of God; true to the indwelling Spirit; true to Christ and to the doctrine concerning him; true to that book of which he is the sum and the burden. Let us be true to *truth*; loving it not because it is pleasant or picturesque or ancient, but *because it is true and divine.* On it let us feed, with appetite new-whetted every day; so shall we add, not one but many cubits to our stature, growing in grace and in the knowledge of our Lord Jesus Christ.[2]

---

2. There is such a thing in the church, as poverty of blood. Hence the blotches that discolour her. For the removal of these, not mere medicine is needed, but a more generous diet. That diet is only to be

Our spiritual constitution must be *braced,* not only that we may be strong for work or fight, but that we may be proof against the infection of the times, against the poison with which the god of this world, 'the prince of the power of the air,' has impregnated our atmosphere. For this we need not only the 'strong meat' recommended by the apostle (Heb. 5:12-14), but the keen fresh mountain-air of trial, vicissitude and hardship; by means of which we shall be made hardy in constitution and robust in frame, impervious to the contagion around, whether that come from ecclesiastical pictorialism or religious liberalism; impregnable against the assaults of Satan the Pharisee, or Satan the Sadducee. They who have slid into a creed (they know not how), or dreamed themselves into it, or been swept into it by the crowd; they to whom the finding of a creed has been a matter of reading, education, or emotion; they to whom faith has been but the result of an *intellectual* conflict, *not a life and death struggle of conscience*; these possess not the true power of resistance; they carry no disinfecting virtue, no error-repelling power about them; the epidemics of the age tell sorely upon them, and even though they may have taken hold of the truth, it becomes evident that the truth has not taken hold of them. In a time of uncertainty, scepticism, speculation, false progress, we

---

found in the word; which is as nourishing (Jer. 15:16) as it is healing and purifying to the blood; being truly what old Tyndale calls it, 'the word of our soul's health'. There is needed, too, the infusion of richer blood, to be brought about by a second Pentecost, in which the existing life will be greatly intensified, and large additions made by conversions of a deeper kind than heretofore. So shall our leanness of faith, of love, of life, of zeal, of joy be efficaciously and abidingly cured. So shall we 'come behind in no gift, waiting for the coming of our Lord Jesus Christ' (1 Cor. 1:7).

need to recognise the full meaning of the apostolic 'we know' (1 John 5:19-20), 'we believe' (2 Cor. 4:13), 'we are confident' (2 Cor. 5:6), 'we are persuaded' (2 Tim. 1:12). For that which is divinely true and certain must be *immortal*. Like the results of the exact sciences, it is fixed; not varying with men and ages. That which *was* true *is* true and *shall be* true for ever. It is the more needful to recognise all this, because the ground underneath us has been thoroughly mined and is very largely hollow; a process of sceptical decomposition and disintegration has been going on, the extent of which will soon be manifest when the treacherous crust gives way.[3]

At the same time let us beware, in the details of personal religion, merely of repeating the past, or getting up an imitation of religion. The genuine in life does not thus repeat itself; nor does it need to do so. The living face of man is a certain type; yet each face varies from its fellow. The Holy Spirit's work is not to form mere statues. He produces *life,* and life is always varied. It is death that repeats itself. As silence is always the same, so is it with death. The presence of life is the security against tame monotony. The larger the infusion of life, the greater the diversity, not of gifts merely, but of beauty and fruit and power. Let us not then seek the living among the dead, nor try to revivify old forms. Let us place ourselves simply

---

3. 'The thoughts of men are widened with the process of the suns,' says the philosophic poet of the age; and the maxim seems accepted. In so far as the widening thoughts are *honest developments* of revelation, the maxim will only express the apostolic 'going on unto perfection,' 'increasing in the knowledge of God.' In so far as they are the results of disengagement from the trammels of revelation, they will express nothing but the progress of uncontrolled free-thinking.

in the hands of the quickening Spirit. He will pour into us the fulness of a diversified, fruitful, healthful life. The evil in us is too strong for any power save Omnipotence. The *resistance of a human will* is too powerful for philosophy or logic, or poetry or eloquence. The Holy One alone can make us holy.

Life is not one battle but many. It is made up, too, of defeats as well as victories. Let us not be unduly troubled or grow moody when a battle is lost. There is always time to win another; and such a thing as flight or 'demoralization' should be unknown in the army of the living God. It is the *lost* battles of the world (like Thermopylae) that have told most on a nation's history. 'If God be for us, who can be against us?' 'Thou hast girded me with strength unto the battle' (Ps. 18:39).

The Christian life is a great thing; one of the greatest things on earth. Made up of daily *littles,* it is yet in itself not a little thing; but in so far as it is truly lived, whether by poor or rich, by child or full-grown man, noble throughout; a part of that great whole, in which and by which is to be made known to the principalities and powers in heavenly places, the manifold wisdom of God (Eph. 3:10).

It does not need to be a *long* life; a short one may be as true and holy as a long one. A short one is not a failure. John the Baptist's was perhaps the shortest ministry in the church; yet it was no failure; it was one of the greatest successes. He was a burning and a shining light. We do not need to say profanely, 'Whom the gods love die young;' but we may say that it does not need the threescore years and ten to unfold the beauties of holiness.

If the new life were the mere rubbing off the rust of the

old; if the sweetening of the Marah-well of our corrupt nature were but a common, non-miraculous process; if all goodness be within the easy reach of any earnest man; if a refined literature and a liberalised theology, and the cultivation of the beautiful, and social science, and a wider range of genial recreations, be the cure for all the evil that is in us and in our age; then there has been much ado about trifles, the Bible is an exaggeration, and the gift of the Holy Spirit a superfluous exhibition of power. If sin be but a common scar or wrinkle, to be erased from the soul's surface by a few simple touches; if pardon be a mere figure of speech, meaning God's wide benevolence or good-natured indifference to evil, why tell of wrath and fire and judgement, the never-dying worm and the ever-rising smoke? Does God love to torment his creatures by harsh words, or fill their imaginations with images of woe which he does not intend to realise? Or why did the Son of God suffer and weep, and grieve? If error be but a trifle, a foible, a freak at worst; or if it be a display of honest purpose and the inevitable result of free thought, why is the 'strong delusion' (literally, 'the energy of error') spoken of so awfully; 'that they all might be damned who believed not the truth' (2 Thess. 2:12); and why did the Lord himself say, once and again, in reference to false doctrine, 'WHICH THING I HATE'? (See Appendix, Note 16).

As the strongest yet calmest thing in the world is *light*, so should a Christian life be the strongest and greatest, as well as the calmest and brightest. As the only perfectly straight line is *a ray of light*, and as the only pure substance is sunshine, so ought our course to be, and so should we seek to shine as lights in the world; reflections of Him who is its light; the one straight, pure thing on earth.

Let us then SHINE! Stars indeed, not suns; but still stars, not tapers nor meteors. Let us *shine*! Giving perhaps slender light, but that light certain and pure; enough to say to men 'it is night,' lest they mistake; but not enough to bring day; enough to guide the seeking or the erring in the true direction, but not enough to illuminate the world. The sun alone can do that. It is *the sun* that shows us the landscape; *stars* show but themselves. Let us then show ourselves beyond mistake. The day when all things shall be seen in full warm light, is the day of the great sun-rising.

'The night is far spent, the day is at hand.' We shall not set nor be clouded; we shall simply lose ourselves in light. And we need not grudge thus losing ourselves, when we call to mind that the splendour in which our light is to be absorbed is that of the everlasting Sun. It is his increasing that is to be our decreasing; and shall we not say, 'This my joy therefore is fulfilled.'

APPENDIX

Note 1 (page 17)
'Ye are clean through *the word* which I have spoken unto you' (John 15:3); that is, made clean through believing *the word*, 'The washing of water by *the word'* (Eph. 5:26[1]); that is, the washing which is accomplished by the belief of *the word*. 'The washing of regeneration' (Tit. 3:5); that is, 'that regeneration which washes us,' not as commonly interpreted, 'that washing which regenerates us,' as is evident from the next clause, 'the renewing of the Holy Ghost,' which signifies not that renewing which gives us the Spirit, but that Spirit which renews us. 'Washed, sanctified, justified' (1 Cor. 6:11); three steps of the great process, making clean, consecrating, making us righteous as Christ is righteous.

Note 2 (page 18)
God's 'fatherhood' is an expression much in use at present, and is assumed by many as a great truth and as the foundation for the liberalized theology of the day. This fatherhood is affirmed to be *universal;* and its universality is made the basis of a new and, as is supposed, a larger gospel. As, to this universal *fatherhood,* the universal *sonship* is the necessary correlative – the preachers of the

---

1. The passage should run thus: 'Christ loved the church and gave himself for it, in order that he might sanctify it (having cleansed it with that washing of water which comes through the word), in order that he might present it to himself, glorious, THE *church* which has no spot nor wrinkle;' that is, *the* church spoken of in the Song of Solomon.

new gospel proclaim to every man that he *is* a son of God, and that it is the belief of this already existing sonship that introduces him into peace.

Now, certain it is that God as *Creator* is *Father*; and that, in this sense, universal fatherhood is a necessary truth; a truth recognised by Scripture – Hebrews 12:9: '*Father* of spirits'; Acts 17:29: 'we are the *offspring* of God'; Luke 3:38: 'Adam, who was the *son* of God'; Malachi 2:10: 'Have we not all *one father*? Hath not one God created us?'; Numbers 16:22: '*The God of the spirits* of all flesh.' Besides this fatherhood of creation there is but one other, that of *redemption.* See John 1:12: 'As many as received him to them gave he power to become the sons of God'; Romans 8:14: 'As many as are led by the Spirit of God, they are the sons of God.' These, and many other passages, show that this sonship begins with faith, and has no existence previously, save in God's eternal purpose.

Incarnation did not make us sons; nay, even *belief in the incarnation does not make us sons;* for the formula, 'he that believeth that *Jesus is the Christ,* is born of God,' includes not incarnation merely, but the whole Messianic character and work. Besides, to affirm that sonship is constituted *previous to faith* is to gainsay the explicit words of Scripture, such as Galatians 3:26: 'ye are all the children of God *by faith* in Christ Jesus'; Galatians 4:5: 'To redeem them that were under the law, that we might receive the adoption of sons'; 2 Corinthians 6:17-18: 'Come out from among them, and be ye separate, and touch not the unclean thing; and I will receive you, and will be a Father unto you, and ye shall be my sons and daughters'; 1 John 3:1: 'Behold what manner of love the Father hath bestowed upon us, that we should be called the sons of God';

Revelation 21:7: 'He that overcometh shall inherit all things; and I will be his God, and he shall be my son.'

I need not cite more passages to show that the 'new birth,' the being 'begotten again', with the sonship consequent on these, is not the universal heritage of humanity, in consequence of the incarnation; but a privilege secured by faith in a *dead* and *risen* Christ (1 Pet. 1:3). To make sonship *co-extensive* with humanity, because of *incarnation,* is to introduce a worse error than that of Thomas Erskine, when he made pardon the universal property of the race, because of the death of Christ. The Bible affirms *creation-sonship,* both in the case of men, as we have seen, and of angels, as we find in Job 38:7 ('the *sons of God* shouted for joy'); and it affirms *redemption-sonship;* but *incarnation-sonship* and its correlative *incarnation-fatherhood* are the figments of human speculation, the rocks of a modern theology, so far 'advanced' as to have distanced, not creeds only, but Scripture itself.

Note 3 (page 31)
The twofold references of certain expressions in Scripture ought to be studied, as the means of clearing up some of the confusion which one-sided teachers propagate. We find, for example, 'redemption,' 'saved,' and 'salvation' used sometimes in reference to the commencement, and sometimes in reference to the consummation of the great deliverance. 'Who *hath* saved us' (2 Tim. 1:9); 'we *shall be* saved' (Rom. 5:10). We find sanctification spoken of sometimes as a thing past and done: 'Ye are sanctified' (1 Cor. 6:11); and sometimes as a thing going on: 'The very God of peace sanctify you wholly' (1 Thess. 5:23). The

old man is sometimes said to have been put off (Col. 3:9) and sometimes Christians are exhorted to put him off (Eph. 4:22). Sometimes that which is new is said to have been accomplished (2 Cor. 5:17), and sometimes the exhortation is given, 'put on the new man' (Eph. 4:24). Sometimes we are spoken of as *having* life (John 3:15), while elsewhere we are told to lay hold on it (1 Tim. 6:12). A Christian is one who has been filled with the Spirit' (Eph. 5:18). Sometimes we are said to have been transformed and renewed (2 Cor. 5:17); at other times we are exhorted to be 'transformed' (Rom. 12:2), and 'renewed' (Eph. 4:23). Sometimes it is said, 'if we say that we have no sin, we deceive ourselves' (1 John 1:8); and sometimes 'whoso abideth in him sinneth not' (1 John 3:6). Sometimes David blesses God for having removed his transgressions from him as far as the east is from the west (Ps. 103:12) and speaks of the blessedness of pardon (Ps. 32:1-5); and again he says, 'pardon mine iniquity' (Ps. 25:11), 'blot out all mine iniquities' (Ps. 51:9). Sometimes the Holy Spirit is referred to as given, once for all, at Pentecost (Acts 2:33); at other times (and this far more frequently) as coming down from time to time in answer to prayer, and along with the preaching of the gospel (Acts 2:38; 4:31; 10:44; 11:15; 19:6). Sometimes we, as those whom Aaron represented, place our hands on the head of the sacrifice, and lay our sins on Christ (Lev. 16:21, 26:40, 1 John 1:9); at other times it is Jehovah that is said to do this (Isa. 53:6).[2] These are but specimens of the *twofold* manner of speech in Scripture, ignorance of which has misled many.

2. Yet the Hebrew word (to strike upon with violence) and the connection, indicate that it is the *punishment* of sin, not sin, that is referred to in this verse of Isaiah.

Note 4 (page 39)

In going to the cross we went with all our guilt, to deposit it where alone it is lawful so to do; to bury it in a grave, out of which there can be no resurrection for it for ever. We gave our heavy burden to God, and he took it from us most lovingly and without a grudge. We 'laid both our hands upon the head' of the great Surety, 'confessing over him all our iniquities and all our transgressions, in all our sins, putting them upon his head'; he 'bearing upon him all our iniquities into a land not inhabited' (Lev. 16:21,22), and we, then, coming into the tabernacle as accepted worshippers (v.23), nay, going into the holiest of all, through the veil that has been rent, to present our worship in 'the cloud of the incense that covers the mercy-seat that is upon the testimony' (v.13).

Having heard the voice that spoke of the great burnt-Sacrifice – the Lamb of God that taketh away the sin of the world – we looked to it, went to it, and laid our sins upon it. That which we then believed was not anything about ourselves save our sin and need; God's testimony to the slain Lamb was the one thing on which our faith rested. We read that 'the Lord hath laid on him the iniquity of us all' (that is, hath inflicted on him our punishment); that the 'chastisement of our peace was upon him' (Isa. 53:5); that 'the Lord was well pleased for his righteousness' sake' (Isa. 42:21); and upon believing the report we realised the transference – our sin passing over to him and his righteousness passing over to us. This was the exchange we made when we believed.

In God's purpose, no doubt, all this was a certainty from eternal ages; and when Christ 'carried up our sins in his own body to the tree' (1 Peter 2:24, see Greek), this purpose began visibly to unfold itself. But this is only the *divine,* not the *human* side of the great question. In the eternal purpose we see God pre-arranging to do certain things when the time for doing them should come; and in the cross we see the righteous provision made for carrying these pre-arrangements into effect. But the human side is that which takes up events as they emerge, and individuals as they come into being and action. Hence the personal transference takes place *upon our believing, not before*; and we might as well speak of eternal conversion and eternal faith as of eternal justification.[3] Both are equally true in one aspect; both are equally untrue in another. The *purpose* to convert and justify belongs to the past eternity; the carrying out of that purpose is an act of time, a fragment of personal human history; and to say, as some do, that because God laid our sins upon Christ from all eternity, therefore it is wrong for us to speak of our doing so in time, is to misuse words, to confound things which differ, to identify the purpose with the execution of the purpose, to obliterate the distinction between the human and the

---

3. Aliud est decretum justificationis, aliud ipsa justificatio, ut aliud est voluntas salvandi et sanctificandi, aliud vero salus et sanctificatio' (Turrentine, Inst. Xvi. 9,3); that is, 'God's justifying decree is one thing, and our actual justification is another.' It is not my belief of the justifying decree that justifies me, nor is it my belief that the Lord laid my sins on Christ eighteen centuries ago, or from the eternal ages, that brings me pardon, but my belief of the faithful saying that Jesus Christ came into the world to save sinners. One-sided statements on this point do much harm; want of clear views as to that very thing which is to be 'most surely believed by us'; mixing up the divine and human, the decree and the fact, and treating the latter as coeval with the former – these have introduced confusion and unsound doctrine, both in our own and former days.

divine, to look at one side only of a subject, forgetting the twofoldness of all truth, specially of that which involves the relations between the finite and the infinite, the unrolling of eternal purposes into events of time. If our sins were so laid on Christ eighteen centuries ago that we do not require to lay them on him now, then of course his righteousness was reckoned to us then; and so we were justified eighteen hundred years before we believed, we were pardoned before we sinned, we were born again before we were born at all.

From the moment we believed, we could count ourselves forgiven men, and God began to deal with us as such. We had learned from the Epistle to the Romans our justification *in law* before God and we learned from the Epistle to the Hebrews our justification *in conscience*, that is, our conscience was 'purged from dead works to serve the living God,' so that we being 'once purged, had no more conscience of sin' (Heb. 10:2). Neither of these things, however, could mean that our *future* sins were *actually* pardoned in the same sense as our past, and at the same time. A sin cannot be *pardoned* till it has been *committed.* If it can be pardoned before being committed, it must be pardoned before it is repented of, or it must be repented of before it is committed, or else repentance and confession are mockeries; and they who speak of all sins, past, present, and to come, being forgiven at once upon believing, are losing sight of the real meaning of words and things, and might as well affirm that we were converted before we were born, or that our disease was cured before we were sick, and that the one act of faith put forth at our conversion is enough for us, without our having recourse to such a lifetime's continuous believing, as is indicated in our Lord's expression, 'He that *believeth* (not has believed) hath everlasting life.' To say that from the day we believed God regards us as forgiven men, men not under wrath but under grace, is one thing; but to say that all our sins are actually pardoned before being committed, is quite another. The apostle certainly did not think that all our future sin was actually pardoned at once, when he said, 'If we confess our sins, he is faithful and just to forgive us our sins' (1 John 1:9); nor did the Lord think so when he taught us to pray, 'Forgive us our debts, as we forgive our debtors,' making daily pardon as needful as daily bread (Matt. 6:11-12).

In John 5:24, where our version has, 'shall not come into *condemnation*,' some would read, 'shall not come into judgement,' contending that it is not possible that they who have died and risen without Christ could ever need to have it said of them that they shall not come into *condemnation,* when they shall not so much as come into *judgement*. But the apostle says elsewhere, '*we* must all stand before the judgement-seat of Christ' (Rom. 14:10); 'so then every one of *us* shall give in his account to God' (Rom. 14:12); *we* must all appear before the judgement-seat of Christ' (2 Cor. 5:10); and in these three passages he is speaking of himself and his fellow-saints. Besides, though the word χριστς (*krisis*) primarily means simply judgement, yet in the New Testament it more frequently signifies 'condemnation'. See Revelation 18:10: 'In one hour is thy *judgement* come'; Revelation 19:2: 'True and righteous are his *judgements*'; John 5:29, 'They that have done evil unto the resurrection of *damnation*' (χριστς); Matthew 23:33: 'How can ye escape the *damnation* of hell.' Thus the refinement on the word χριστς comes to nothing, having no basis either of Scripture or criticism to rest upon. No less unscriptural is the refinement of some, that the saints are to stand before the judgement-seat of *Christ*, and the world before the Judgement-seat of the *Son of Man*. To say that this is a distinction without a difference might suffice, but the distinction is negatived by the very passage quoted (Rom. 14:10), which quotation is from Isaiah 44:23 where the reference is clearly to the world in general. Besides, how is a saint to be recompensed for his *bad* deeds (2 Cor. 5:19). Is the judgement-seat of Christ for the *punishment* of the saints?

Note 5 (page 54)
I need not quote much from the classics to prove the above; that touching passage from the old Roman poet is enough. It shows the best dies of Paganism:

'Non es avarus? Abi. Quid, caetera jam simul isto
Cum vito fugêre? Caret tibi pectus inani
Ambitione? Caret mortis formidine et ara,' etc. – *Hor.* Ep. II:2.

The whole eight lines we venture to translate for the unlearned reader:

> You love not gold? 'Tis well. Has every sin
> Vanished, with avarice, from its seat within?
> Ambition, has it perished from your breast?
> Is dread of death, is passion all at rest?
> At dreams, spells, portents, wizards, can you smile;
> The nightly spectre, the Thessalian wile?
> Thy birthdays count'st thou with a grateful mind,
> To friends are thou forgiving still and kind?
> Art thou, as age upon thy front appears,
> Gentler, and better with declining years?
> What 'vails one thorn pluckt up, one evil slain,
> If in thy breast ten thousand yet remain?

Note 6 (page 59)

There are some among us who shrink from what they call 'strong statements' on the doctrine of free and immediate justification. They say that they fear the effect which such statements may have on sanctification, and they protest, in the name of morality, against the idea of such an unconditional justification, as would exclude the sinner from any share whatever in working it out. To us it appears that unconditional justification is the real basis of all morality, and that any attempt to give man a share in helping on the justifying process is destructive, we do not say of morality merely, but of *the power to become moral.* No justification will truly serve the interests of morality, save that which at once places the sinner on a footing in which he can do good works, such as God will accept; in other words, any justification that would result in good works must first deal with the *person* who is to work them. The harp must be tuned before it can play, and it would be folly to speak of *playing it into tune*. So the person must be justified before one good work can be done. Our consciences must first be purged by the blood before we can serve God acceptably; and they are to be purged, not only from the works which in themselves are bad, but from 'dead works' (Heb. 9:14), that is, from works which, good in their own nature, are without life, because done by one whose conscience is not pacified towards God.

The homilies of the Church of England state this well:

'Faith giveth life to the soul; and they be as much dead to God that lack faith, as they be to the world whose bodies lack souls. Without faith, all that is done of us is but dead before God, although the works seem never so gay and glorious before man. They do appear to be lively works, and indeed they be but dead, not availing to the everlasting life; they be but shadows and shows of lively and good things, and not good and lively things indeed. For true faith does give life to the works; and out of such faith come good works, that be very good works indeed, and without faith no work is good before God. We must set no good works before faith, nor think that before faith a man may do any good works; for such works, although they seem unto men to be praiseworthy, yet indeed they be but vain, and not allowed before God. Faith is that which does commend the work to God; for as St. Augustine saith, whether thou wilt or no, that work that cometh not of faith is naught; where the faith of Christ is not the foundation, there is no good work, what building soever we make.... All the life of them that lack the true faith is sin. As soon as a man hath faith, even he shall flourish in good works; for faith of itself is full of good works, and nothing is good without faith.... As men, that be very men indeed, first have life, and afterwards be nourished; so must our faith in Christ go before, and afterwards be nourished by good works; but first he must have faith.... Faith by itself saved him (the thief), but works by themselves never justified any man' (Sermon of Good Works).

There are some in our day who, while denying imputed righteousness, would, in a certain sense, acquiesce in the above statements. They would say that a man must trust God before he can do good works. But then they hold:

(1) that the doing of good works necessarily indicates faith already existing.

(2) Faith is in their theology merely a right state of mind toward God.

(3) Our recognition of the universal fatherhood of God fits us for doing good works.

(4) We do not need to be judicially or forensically justified, because we were never in that sense condemned.

(5) In so far as any justification is needed, it was accomplished for every man when the Son of God took flesh; and faith is simply our coming to know that such is the case.

(6) Any other *personal* justification is simply God acknowledging and rewarding the good deeds done by those who trust his fatherhood, and refuse to believe that he could be so stern a judge as to demand life for life, in order to the pardon of a sinner. God's character, as judge, has no place in their theology. Hence his dealings with sin are not judicial or legal; and his actings about pardon are not forensic, but fatherly, or rather the result of what in man would be called good-natured softness, and easy-minded indifference to the distinctions of moral rectitude.

But the faith which is the parent or root of good works is not a mere change of opinion or heart as to the character of God, though it includes this. It is the belief of something *which is designed to alter the man's legal standing,* as well as his state of feeling; for before a man can do good works it is quite as indispensable that his *condemnation should be reversed, and his conscience pacified,* as that his thoughts of God should be set right. To those who believe that the sinner never was under condemnation, or under wrath; but that all his uneasiness arose from not knowing that there is *no such thing as condemnation* or wrath; the above statement may seem an absurdity; but to those who take such expressions as these – sin and guilt and wrath and condemnation and judgement – in their natural and literal sense, a judicial acquittal from a legal charge, a judicial pardon of a judicial sentence, in consequence of believing God's testimony to the work of the Substitute, will be recognised as that without which the sinner is not in a position to do good works, nor in circumstances even to begin to be holy.

The Romish doctors and creeds do not go quite so far astray. They believe in guilt and condemnation and pardon; and though they mix up the judicial and the moral, the sinner's standing and the sinner's character, the work for us and the work in us, they recognise the judicial element as constituting the basis of the moral, and do not so ignore the teachings of Scripture as to depict their Deity as a God of benevolent weakness, such as the 'advanced theologians,' imbibing as far as may be considered safe the subtle infidelities of the age, are now learning to do. Romanists have always held that sin and pardon were real things, and matters for judicial action, though the *grounds* of the judgement they have thoroughly mis-stated. The modern theologians referred to have withdrawn sin and pardon from the judgement-seat altogether, and yet, strange to say, have retained much of the Romish confusion, and on the point of justification have adopted a creed more Trentine than Trent itself.

Rome holds that we are justified by *infused* right-eousness, but then she holds that this is in consequence of Christ having satisfied divine justice by his death. The advanced theology maintains that the ideal of such a satisfaction is an affront to the divine fatherhood; and that, as it is only from sin, *as a disease,* that we need deliverance, our one remedy is assimilation to God by belief and contemplation of his fatherhood, to which deliverance the belief in a judicial pardon, founded on a legal substitution, is a fatal hindrance, not a help at all. Thomas Erskine started this thought in his work on the unconditional freeness of the gospel. John Campbell took it up and enforced it from the pulpit. Edward Irving wrought it into his later theology and expounded it at length. Maurice, Kingsley and the recent divines of progress have been indebted to these three for all that is essential and attractive in their systems. The righteousness for which God accepts us is (writes Irving)

> 'a real substantial purification of soul and body, but not self-originated, not self-supplied, derived all from Christ, by him wrought out, and out of him derived to us. Like other precious truths, Satan hath converted this to his own false and unholy uses, making men believe that, because it is derived from Christ, and by him sustained, it is therefore not really a righteousness *wrought in us,* but only a garment covering us, and that withal we continue under the cloak to be the same filthy creatures as before, whom God, for Christ's sake (as they, with seeming piety, express a most impious sentiment) is pleased to look upon as righteous. If this be what they mean by the doctrine of imputed righteousness, and it is what they commonly express, then it is the vilest of all vile doctrines, comforting and encouraging a sinner in his wickedness under the false notion that faith entirely covers and protects sin from the judgement of God. The church never meant to assert that, because it was of Christ's working out for us and of God's serving out to us, it was not therefore true righteousness, heart righteousness, righteousness in the inward parts, and in the outward also, holiness of body and holiness of soul. The church never meant to convey by the word "imputed" that the righteousness was only skin deep, or, if we may so speak,

only cloak deep, while all beneath was as foul as ever, or that it was only a supposititious righteousness, and not a real and substantial, or that it was only a transfer done over from Christ's folio, in the great book of accounts, to ours.'[4]

From the above extracts the reader will see whence the 'new school' theology of the present day gathered their denunciations of the 'legal fiction' of imputation, though they have gone far beyond their teacher. Of the subtle deism underlying these attacks on substitution and judicial dealing with the sinner, and this zeal for the universal fatherhood of God, combined with denial of full inspiration, that is, of *divine accuracy*, to the language of Scripture, this is not the place to speak. But one would be disposed to argue that the fatherhood of a being who allowed his children to pine away with poverty and grief for six thousand years, when he might have made them all so happy; who gave them as his only expression of sympathy, and their only guide, a miserably imperfect volume, with hardly one word in it which they can strictly call his own, is an idea, a myth, which they themselves can only believe in as a refuge from the dreary negations

---

4. Irving on the Revelation, vol. 2, pp. 889, 890. The author of the above must have forgotten that he had subscribed a confession which teaches that 'those whom God effectually calleth, he also freely justifieth, not by infusing righteousness into them, but by pardoning their sins, and by *accounting and accepting their persons as righteous, not for anything wrought in them or done by them,* but for Christ's sake alone; not by imputing faith itself, the act of believing, or any other evangelical obedience to them as their righteousness, but by *imputing the obedience and satisfaction of Christ unto them.* Christ, by his obedience and death, did *fully discharge the debt of* all who are thus justified, and did make a proper, real and full satisfaction to his Father's justice in their behalf' (Westminster Confession, Ch.xi).

into which they are step by step descending. Let them who believe in God's universal fatherhood say if such a half-inspired and inaccurate Bible, as they will have it to be, is worthy of such a Father.

In our conflict with sin and pursuit of holiness, we must take our stand, not upon sensations or intuitions or impulses, or the experiences of others, but upon a true and accurate Bible, one for whose truth and accuracy we have divine security. If in that Bible we have merely the words of a man sketching and illustrating and abridging the thoughts of God, we have no security for the absolute correctness of any one statement in Scripture; and therefore no foundation for faith to rest on. Our ideas of sin and pardon and holiness must be mere guesses, approximations to the truth it may be, no more. Peace with God, consciousness of pardon, sense of reconciliation, become impossibilities. For the resting-place of the soul as to these, and the one basis of faith as to all religious truth, is the naked word of him that cannot lie.

The sinner asks the question, 'Wherewith shall I come before the Lord?' and God answers it *in his own words.* On these words we rest, in drawing near to God. He whose conscience has never asked this question in thorough earnest may be content with any response, however indefinite, and conveyed in words, however loose and vague; but he who has put it forth from the depths of his trembling spirit will be satisfied with no answer that does not come straight from the lips of God.

Note 7 (page 60)
To say that assurance of one's salvation is of the essence of faith, and that is the *first* part of the gospel, is to depart

from Scripture as much as from common sense. For to believe that I am saved before I am saved, or to be sure that I am pardoned in order to be pardoned, is a contradiction such as only incoherency could announce. But to say that assurance of salvation is the immediate and necessary *result* of faith is to follow the teaching of the apostles, and to give the true interpretation to their gospel. For if the belief of that gospel does not forthwith assure me of my own acceptance, it must make me thoroughly miserable. The more that its blessings are apprehended, the more wretched must I become, if it can bring me no *present* certainty as to my share in these; if the first result of my *believing* it is to land me in an interval of *doubt*, from which I can only extricate myself by years of effort. To keep a prisoner waiting for twenty years in his cell before assuring him of the royal pardon would not be half so cruel as to keep the awakened sinner for a day uncertain as to the pardon of his sin. Every hour's uncertainty would be a foretaste of hell. Yet this uncertainty is all the good news which many preach. They proclaim a gospel which merely sets the sinner a working for salvation, a *trying* to believe! They tell him that if he will only go on thus, doing his best and trying to believe, for twenty or thirty years, God will take pity upon his laborious endeavours and show favour to his earnestness! They call on him to sum up his good feelings at certain seasons, and on that summation to build his hope of becoming by degrees at last an accepted man! But all the while what is the poor soul to do, with an awakened conscience, and terrors of doom, and thoughts of the possibility of being lost after all? This surely is not the gospel of Christ and his apostles. It is not the gospel which brought such *immediate* joy, *as soon as believed*, to the sinners of Jerusalem, Antioch and Philippi. It contains no good news, because no certainty of pardon to the sinner, no present purging of the conscience through the blood.

The want of assurance has frequently been defended from the Psalms. On this point we suggest the following thoughts:

There are two extremes of interpretation in the case of the Psalms. The first almost sets aside Christ from them, and understands the expressions of bitterness and grief as merely David's utterances; as oftentimes the utterances of doubt, and unbelief, and want of assurance. That they were the utterances of David's feelings in the circumstances in which they were composed, is most true, and ought to be taken as the basis of all interpretations; but that they were not meant by the Holy Spirit for a greater than David is a serious error; that they are the utterances of doubt, or unbelief, or non-assurance, or want of faith, is even a more serious error, for not only does it make the Holy Spirit put words of distrust into a believer's lips (nay, we should say, into Messiah's lips), but it overlooks this notable fact that even those psalms which are darkest throughout, and read most like doubting, begin with 'My God,' or similar words of assurance; nay, that the very bitterness expressed is occasioned by the thought that this God, about whose relationship to them no doubt is entertained, is giving them over to the will of their enemies.

The second interpretation exhibits Christ in them as the true speaker, though the voice and pen at first were David's. But though this seems to us, speaking generally, the correct view, we should not like to see it supersede the use of the Psalms by Christians as in many parts expressive of New Testament experiences as truly as of Old. To speak of Jewish saints as occupying lower ground and inheriting a lower kingdom than we do, or as liable to an experience of conflict from which we have been delivered, is to exhibit a one-sidedness of view and an ignorance of the Christian warfare hardly to be expected in men who have studied the whole Word of God. To tear away the Psalms from us as obsolete, and to deny them to be the proper utterance of Christian worship because of the sorrow which breathes through so many of them, is to deprive us of the means of identifying ourselves with Old Testament saints, and to shut us out from the use of language which best embodies the feelings of one wrestling, not with flesh and blood, but with principalities, and powers; and of one who 'groans, being burdened' (2 Cor. 5:4), is in 'heaviness through manifold temptations' (1 Peter 1:6), oppressed with 'infirmities,' pierced with 'thorns in the flesh' and buffeted by messengers of Satan (2 Cor. 12:7-10); troubled on every side, fightings without and fears within (2 Cor. 7:5). Let those who have soared above Paul and David, who call conflict bondage, and treat the cries of Old Testament saints as something which it would be sin for us to listen to, reject the Psalms and their experiences; those who know something of the warfare will welcome them as suitable and precious above measure – the breathings, not of the spirit of bondage, but of liberty and adoption.

Note 8 (page 65)

It will contribute to some clearness of thought, on this point, to bring together the passages which speak of the new and old man. They are the following:

(1) Colossians 3:9-10: 'Ye have put off the *old man* with his deeds; and have put on the *new man*.' If , then, the whole old man (in a moral sense) be *literally* put off, and the new put on, the man is perfect, sinless.

(2) 2 Corinthians 5:17: 'If any man be in Christ, he is a *new creature*; old things are passed away; behold, all things are become new.' How then does the 'old man' still remain, unchanged, and unchangeable?

(3) Galatians 6:15: 'In Christ Jesus neither circumcision availeth anything, nor uncircumcision, but a *new creature*,' i.e. the whole man is created anew.

(4) Ephesians 2:15: 'To make in himself of twain *one new man.*

(5) Ephesians 4:22-24, 'That ye put off the *old man*; .. and be *renewed* in the spirit of your mind; and put on the *new man.*'

(6) Romans 6:6: 'Our *old man* is crucified with him.' Are there no figures here? Or is not the purging out of the *old leaven* a figure (1 Cor. 5:7)? Is not 'the putting on of Christ' a figure (Rom. 13:14)? Is not the 'putting on of bowels and mercies' a figure (Col. 3:12)?

Through the putting off the old and putting on the new man is in one sense *an act* done once at justification; yet that there is an inner work flowing from this is evident from the expression, 'the inner man is *renewed day by day*,' and the exhortation to the *saints,* 'put ye on the Lord Jesus Christ' (Rom. 13:14); while it is said elsewhere, 'as many as have been baptized into Christ have put on Christ' (Gal. 3:27). In one sense then the change is complete ('ye are complete in him'); in another it is incomplete. Nor is there any contradiction here, but only *two sides* of one great truth, which some overlooking have erred from the faith, and said strange things concerning flesh and spirit, the old man and the new man, which Scripture warrants not; all founded upon a one-sided view of truth, and defended by carrying out literally and extremely the *figures* of the apostles and our Lord.

One figure used is that of an indwelling Christ. 'Christ in you' (Col. 1:27); 'Christ liveth in me' (Gal. 2:20); 'that Christ may dwell in your hearts by faith' (Eph. 3:17); 'I will come in to him, and sup with him' (Rev. 3:20). But Christ is in heaven, and therefore cannot actually dwell in us, body, soul, spirit, and Godhead, as the Romanists maintain regarding the sacrament of the supper. Everything that Christ could do for us and be to us, if he were actually inhabiting us, *that* is implied by this figure of an indwelling Christ, as done for us and in us. The language is figurative; and the apostle did not mean that the new man in us is Christ himself.

Another figure used is that of the Holy Spirit making us his temples, his habitations. Certainly he does dwell in us and fill us; he occupies us as his temples in so far as Godhead can inhabit man. But there is a limit to the use of the figure. The Holy Spirit is not the same as the new man, nor does he make in us a new personality; but occupies us in every part, and, in occupying, transforms and purifies. He does not create a new individual, spotlessly pure like himself, and insert it into us, leaving the whole of our old being untouched and unchanged, to wage warfare with the new individual which has been thus dropped into us. What he does is to quicken the man, be it Abraham or Paul or Luther; to renew the man, the whole man the whole of this Abraham, this Paul, this Luther, so that though renewed in every part, spirit, soul, and body, he is still very Abraham, very Paul, very Luther, just as before.

Note 9 (page 66)
Let us note this passage more especially, because of its importance. The apostle says, in Galatians 2:19: 'I through the law am dead (died) to the law, that (in order that) I might live unto God.' But how or when did he die to the law? How or when did the law slay him? When he became one with Christ in his death. As the law slew his substitute, so did it in that act slay himself. As the power of the law over his substitute ceased when he died and paid the penalty, so did it cease in reference to himself when he became one with him who died. Thus, Paul died to the law in order that he might live unto God. But how, and where, and when did this death of Paul take place? On the cross. In God's purpose, and in the eye of his law, all who should throughout the ages believe in Jesus are looked upon as gathered into one around the cross, when Jesus was fixed to it, nay, nailed to the cross with him. Hence Paul as one of that company says, 'I have been crucified with Christ.' Yes, Paul, the whole Paul, was crucified. But Paul, the very Paul, is yet alive. The crucified man lives! He rose with his 'Surety'; with him who was 'delivered for our offences' (or rather, 'because we had sinned'), and raised again for 'our justification' (or rather, 'because we were justified'). There is a change, not in the *person,* for he is still Paul; but in the nature of the person. He has got a new life, new feelings, and new capacity of feeling, new sympathies, new sorrows, and new joys, new loves, and new hatreds, and this newness is through an indwelling Christ. Paul is now alive through the vitality

of another life than his own; strong through the strength of another; wise through the wisdom of another; holy through the holiness of another. He thinks, feels and acts through the energy of another. Hence the apparent contradiction of the 'I live, yet not I'; 'I, yet not I, but the grace of God that is in me.'

Note 10 (page 75)

God, in the record of his dealings with the Old Testament saints, leads us to connect all blessing specially with HIMSELF.

He speaks of *himself*, not merely as *giving* the blessing; or as being the source of it; but as *being* the blessing: *being* it, in such a way that he who has him has all of blessing that is in him; *being* it, in such a way that the only means of getting it is by getting himself. What he is and has is the exponent of the *nature* and the measure of the *amount* of blessing.

Men call this a mere figure of speech. Be it so. It is a figure which, with all its boldness, falls far short of the real thing which God would have us understand by it; for human speech, though strained to the utmost, cannot adequately utter the great thoughts of God.

When God would give Abraham the promise of security here and recompense hereafter, he does not simply say, 'I will protect and reward thee.' He says far more, 'I am thy shield, and thy exceeding great reward' (Gen. 15:1). And when he reminds Israel of their dependence on him, he says: 'He is thy life, and the length of thy days' (Deut. 30:20). To say God is my 'treasure', my 'rock', my 'fortress', my 'light', the 'health of my countenance', is not only to make use of a more 'poetical' expression; but it is to utter a far greater and more blessed truth than to say, God enriches me, defends me, enlightens me, heals me.

In the New Testament we have the same form of speech; and there it becomes even more expressive, because it is made use of in connection with the person and work of the Son of God, with him in whom it hath pleased the Father that all fulness should dwell. Related as he is to us, and we to him – he the Word made flesh and we the members of his body; he partaker of our true and real humanity and we the 'partakers of the divine nature' – it may be said that the 'figures' above referred to assume a personality, a meaning and a power such as they never before possessed. In Jesus Christ – who is at once the substitute, the surety, the sacrifice, the sin-bearer, and no less the brightness of Jehovah's glory and the express image of his person – all these forms of speech find their true filling up and complete significance. 'I am the resurrection and the life', 'I am the light of the world', 'I am the bread of life', 'I am the way, and the truth and the life', he says of himself. And his apostles say of him, 'He is our peace,' 'He of God is made unto us wisdom, and righteousness, and sanctification, and redemption.' All that he is and has of life, peace, wisdom, righteousness, sanctification, redemption, are ours; for he is ours, and we are his; we are 'made partakers of Christ', one with him in all that he possesses, or of which he is the heir.

Christ is 'our peace', for that which he *is* and *has* and *has done* secures our reconciliation with God; and in the knowledge of him and his propitiation, we are delivered from all disquietude and dread of wrath, once and for ever; God is at peace with us, and we at peace with God.

'Christ is the wisdom of God' and he 'of God is made unto us wisdom'. This does not mean that Christ is the divine attribute of wisdom, or that he is made unto us this divine attribute, or that this divine attribute becomes ours, as some would have us to infer. It means that all the wisdom of Godhead is embodied and exhibited in Christ's person and work, nay, is deposited in him as a fountain for us. All that Christ is and has, as the wisdom of God, is placed at our disposal. In him are hid all the treasures of wisdom and knowledge; out of his fulness we all receive; we are 'wise in Christ'. As partakers of himself, we are made partakers of his wisdom. Our heritage from the first Adam is foolishness, from the last is wisdom.

Christ is 'the righteousness of God' and he 'of God is made unto us righteousness'. As the term 'the wisdom of God' did not mean the divine attribute of wisdom; so, as we have seen, 'the righteousness of God' cannot mean the divine attribute of righteousness. It must mean something communicable, something transferable, something of which we become possessors in being made 'partakers of Christ', something in regard to which a legal exchange takes place between us and him: 'He was made sin for us, that we might be made the righteousness of God in him.' Of course, there is a difference here between the way in which the wisdom and the righteousness are applied to us. Wisdom cannot be *imputed* to us, save in the sense of all our foolishness being covered, and we regarded by God as one with him who is wisdom. But righteousness can be imputed; so imputed that the law will treat us as righteous; so imputed that God will deal with us as entitled to all that his righteous Son is entitled to. In being identified with the Righteous One, with him who is the Lord our Righteousness, we receive all the favour and love and blessing and recompense, here and hereafter, which he, as the Righteous One, can claim from the Father. Our sin is transferred to his account, his righteousness to ours. Being thus legally justified, the inward process begins and we are gradually made by the Holy Spirit inwardly that which we are in law by 'the righteousness of Jesus Christ our Saviour'. The two things are inseparable, the legal and the moral, the outward and the inward. It is vain to talk of an inward holiness, of which the root is not justification through the righteousness of the substitute; and it is no less vain to speak of a justification of which the fruit is not inward holiness, the renovation of the whole being.

Christ 'of God is made unto us sanctification'. Some from this have inferred that there is such a thing as imputed sanctification. If they merely mean that, as one with Christ, the Holy One of God, we are treated by God as once set apart for his service, they affirm nothing new. If they assert that, in consequence of Christ being our sanctification, our sins are no longer accounted sins, whatever we may do, then they are the enemies of all godliness and the advocates of crime. If by that which they call perfect sanctification, they simply mean complete consecration, like that of the priests of old, through the blood, they are playing with words and confounding simple minds. Every believer in the blood of Christ holds 'perfect sanctification,' in the sense of every believer being 'a saint,' a 'sanctified' one; one set apart for God and his service, by the sprinkling of the blood, from the moment he believes. But perfect sanctification, in the sense of perfect freedom from sin, from the moment of believing, is nowhere taught in Scripture. One-sided teachers may mystify the minds of the simple by appealing to this and the other passage of Scripture, but let the distinction above adverted to between consecration and holiness be adverted to, and the mystification vanishes.

Some have held that the expression 'the righteousness of God' (Rom. 1:17) means merely 'God's method of justification' – a very meagre, to say the least of it, equivalent for such a powerful phrase. Others have held that it means God's attribute of righteousness itself; an interpretation as unscriptural as it is wholly unintelligible; an interpretation which by refusing to identify the exhibition of God's righteousness with the life of the Son of God on earth, deprives us of that gospel which bases itself on the imputation of the sinner's sin to the substitute, and of the substitute's righteousness to the sinner. If, by 'the righteousness of God' the apostle meant the divine attribute of righteousness, then his reasoning as to the disobedience of the first Adam and the obedience of the second is a fallacy throughout; his gospel is made void; the mutual transference of sin and righteousness between the sinner and the Sin-bearer is set aside; and Luther's joyous gospel of 'Christ our righteousness' is proved to be a poor human fiction, a false gospel, which spoke of peace to the sinner when there was none. Let us test the meaning by a few texts:

2 Corinthians 5:21: 'He, who knew no sin; was made sin for us, that we might be made the righteousness of God in him;' Are we made the divine attribute of righteousness? Or does that attribute become ours?

Romans 1:17: 'Therein (in the gospel) is the righteousness of God revealed from faith to faith.' Is it the divine attribute of righteousness that the gospel reveals to faith?

Romans 3:22: 'The righteousness of God which is by faith of Jesus Christ.' Can this mean the divine attribute of righteousness? Or in what sense is it by faith of Christ?

Romans 5:17, 'They which receive the abundance of grace, and of the gift of righteousness.' How can we receive the abundance of the gift of the divine attribute of righteousness?

Romans 10:3: 'Have not submitted themselves to the righteousness of God.' This cannot mean that they have not submitted to the divine attribute of righteousness.

This 'righteousness of God' is clearly that referred to in Jeremiah 23:6: 'This is the name by which he shall be called, Jehovah our righteousness'; in Daniel 9:24: 'Brought in everlasting righteousness'; Isaiah 61:10: 'He hath covered me with the robe of righteousness'; Romans 10:4: 'Christ is the end of the law for righteousness to every one that believeth'; 2 Peter 1:1: 'The righteousness of God and our Saviour Jesus Christ'; Romans 5:19: 'As by one man's disobedience many were made sinners, so by the obedience of one shall many be made righteous.' These quotations prove that by 'the righteousness of God', the apostle did not mean the divine perfection of righteousness, but the embodiment of obedience seen in the surety life and death of Christ. God, in and by the life and death of his incarnate Son, provided that righteousness which is called 'the righteousness of God'; not simply because it is the righteousness of Christ, who is God, but because it is the righteousness provided, recognised, approved by *God*; and so distinguished from and contrasted with that got up and approved by *man*; as the apostle distinguishes them, 'That I may be found IN HIM (not in myself); not having mine own righteousness which is of the law (which comes by the doing of the law), but that which is through the faith of Christ (which comes by believing in Christ); even the righteousness which is of God by faith.'

Note 11 (page 98)

There seems to be some confusion as to the meaning of 'flesh' in this theory; or something of the old Manichaean doctrine as to the necessary sinfulness of 'flesh'. Flesh in Scripture is used figuratively, (1) for the body (Col. 2:1); (2) the man as he was before conversion, legally and morally (Eph. 2:3); (3) that part or element in the regenerate man which is not yet purified (Rom. 7:25). Nowhere does Scripture speak of some mysterious person called the old man as an unchanged and unchangeable being. It rather speaks thus as to the way in which we are to deal with that which it, in figure, calls the flesh, 'mortify your members which are upon the earth' (Col. 2:5). Whose members? Those of the 'old man' or flesh, such as forni-cation, uncleanness, covetousness; 'ye put off all these, anger, wrath ...'; 'lie not one to another, seeing ye have put off the old man with his deeds'; which texts imply that there is a gradual 'mortifying' or getting quit of what belonged to the old man, which is to continue until we have got rid of all his deeds. The source of this strength against sin, of this daily victory over the lusts of the flesh, *is that which was done to the old man when we were crucified with Christ,* and when we *ceased to seek justifi-cation from the doings of the natural man* (see Haldane on the Romans, and his remarks on the 8th chapter) – or, as the apostle expresses it, ceased to have 'confidence in the flesh' (Phil. 3:3). The crucifying or putting off the old man is *the setting aside of our old self,* as condemned, sentenced, punished in Christ. Just as the *law* was set aside in the matter of our pardon; so was *self,* which was the doer of the law and the seeker of justification through these doings. Both *law* and *self* were nailed to the cross; not in order to be *annihilated;* but to come forth in a new form, the one to be the rule of a holy life and the other to be the doer of holy deeds. Thus 'the law of the Spirit of life in Christ Jesus makes us free from the law of sin and death'. The crucifixion or putting off the flesh or old man *refers primarily to justification*; to our *legal,* not our *moral* state. So long as our old self was at work, it could only bring forth its own fruits; but when we renounced both it and the law (in the matter of pardon), we became attached to a new root, and came under a new influence, for the bringing forth of new fruits. In the statement that the old man is unchangeable, the reference must be to *legal* condition, not *moral* character.

Note 12 (pages 92, 112)

In this passage (1 Cor. 9:21), the apostle brings out his relationship to the law very pointedly.. He was not ὑπο νομον *(upo nomon),* 'under the law' (verse 20); nor was he ἄνομος *(anomos),* 'without law;' but he was ἔννομος *(ennomos),* 'in the law,' or 'subject to the law,' as the word means. See Acts 19:39: 'A lawful assembly,' *i.e.* an assembly regulated by law. A Christian man then is ἔννομος, A MAN NOT 'UNDER THE LAW,' BUT 'WITHIN THE CIRCLE OF LAW.' It is 'to Christ' that he is now 'in law;' but this implies, not an altered law, but the same law placed on a new footing, enforced with new motives; issuing not from Sinai, but from Sion. The 'law of Christ' (Gal. 6:2) is not opposed to the 'law of God,' but a carrying out of all its precepts. Hence the apostolic injunction here, 'Bear ye one another's burdens,' is only a new and more specific application of 'Thou shalt love thy neighbour as thyself.' As in the 5th and 6th chapters of Matthew, the Lord took the law and brought out all its breadth (and what he said to his disciples he says to us), so the apostle here makes a similar use and application of the law; not adding something which the law had omitted, but *drawing out of the law* the holy riches which it contained; and thereby rendering it almost impossible for any one to say, 'We have nothing to do with the law.' Nothing to do with statutes so full of holiness, so fraught with love! As the Lord and his apostles thus illustrated and applied the law, so let us learn to do. To shrink from the law looks very like loving the darkness rather than the light, very like an unwillingness to be instructed in the ways of righteousness. 'I will put *my laws* into their mind' (Heb. 8:10) is connected with 'their sins and their iniquities will I remember no more'; and he who knows forgiveness best and most will not reckon this a return to legalism or bondage. It is the essence of the glorious liberty of the latter day; a part of the *new* covenant (Jer. 31:31; Heb. 8:6-13). This new or 'everlasting covenant' is that which the cross completed, which the blood sealed, and which at Pentecost was so fully proclaimed.

We cannot get our consciences enlightened, or our steps guided straightly, or ourselves taught the full knowledge of good and evil, without the good and holy law of God. 'I had not known sin but by the law: for I had not known lust, except the law had said, Thou shalt not covet' (Rom. 7:7); 'by the law is the knowledge of sin'; 'that sin by the commandment might become exceeding sinful' (Rom. 7:13). That the life of Christ is the embodiment and exposition of the law is true; but it is to be remembered that the four Gospels do not contain the thousandth part of the life of Christ (John 21:25); and that therefore there are many parts and details of the law on which the *revealed* life of Christ does not bear. We are not therefore to confine ourselves to the incidents of his life; nor to say that unless we find such and such a precept exemplified in his life, we are not bound to obey it, which would be the case were it true that Christ's example is to us a substitute for the law. It is far amiss to say we are not to learn the evil of sin from the law but the cross alone. We must have both; the law to teach us what sin is, the cross to teach us the condemnation attaching to it.

God's appeal to Israel in behalf of his laws and statutes are not to be evaded by us. They were addressed by a redeeming God to a redeemed people, that 'knew the joyful sound' (Ps. 89:15), and had tasted the blessedness of pardon. These appeals were not meant to bring them into bondage. Obedience was liberty to them as to us. Israel stood upon the blood, just as we do. Abraham is Paul's model of a justified man; and David his model of a man enjoying the blessedness of righteousness without works. The freest proclamations of pardon and life, in which *we* rejoice, are those addressed to Israel. Old Testament believers did not occupy a lower level than we do; nor did they walk in legal bondage because they had not yet seen the cross. They were 'saints' as truly as we are[5] (Exod. 19:6; Lev. 11:44; 19:2; Deut. 33:3; Ps. 89:5-7); dwelt in,

---

5. The words of the apostle are very explicit. The 'far off' Gentiles were not only to be brought nigh, but to be made 'fellow-citizens *with the saints,* and of the household of God' (Eph. 2:19); *i.e.* fellow-citizens of the heavenly city, *along with all the saints of old.*

and filled with the Holy Spirit (Exod. 28:3, 31:3; 35:31; Num. 11:17,25; 2 Sam. 23:2; Prov. 1:23; Isa. 44:3; 63:11; Mic. 3:.8; 2 Peter 1:21); sons of God (Exod. 4:22-23; Prov. 3:11; Jer. 31:9, 20; Hos. 1:10; Heb. 12:5); God's royal priesthood (Exod. 19:6); God's portion and inheritance (Deut. 32:9); heirs of the kingdom of heaven (Matt. 8:11); strangers upon earth (1 Chron. 29:15; Ps. 39:12; Heb. 11:13); partakers of the first resurrection (Heb. 11:35); members of Christ's body (Isa. 54:5, 62:5); partakers of the heavenly calling (Heb. 11:10, 16). In short, there is nothing affirmed of New Testament saints that is not affirmed of Old Testament ones; and to say that because Israel *as a nation* had the *earthly things,* therefore *the saints in Israel* had not the *heavenly,* is to overlook some of the clearest declarations of the word. The mystery or secret which the apostle announces (Eph. 3:6) was not that a new thing called the church had commenced at Pentecost (there is no hint of such a thing), but that into the *old and well known body,* THE CHURCH, so often spoken of in the Old Testament, and symbolized in the Song of Solomon as THE *church without spot or wrinkle* (Cant. 4:7), the Gentiles were to be introduced and set on the same level as the Old Testament members. 'That the Gentiles should be *fellow-heirs* (with the ancient saints), and of the *same body*' (with them), is the fair interpretation of the apostle's language.

Note 13 (page 110)

The word which our translators render 'sound doctrine' is, properly, healthful or healing doctrine, $\dot{v}\gamma\iota\alpha\iota\nuο\upsilon\sigma\alpha$ $\delta\iota\delta\alpha\sigma\kappa\alpha\lambda\iota\alpha$ *(ugiainousa didaskalia).* It occurs several times: 1 Timothy 1:10: 'Contrary to *healing* doctrine'; 1 Timothy 6:3: 'And consent not to *healing* words;' 2 Timothy 1:13: 'Hold fast the form of *healing* words'; 2 Timothy 4:3: 'They will not endure *healing* doctrine.' See Titus 1:9, 13; 2:1-2. The doctrine that heals the soul's hurt, is Paul's faithful saying. Everything else but heals it slightly, or introduces poison into the wound. It is remarkable that this is the word by which the Greek translators of the Old Testament have rendered the Hebrew word 'peace'. See Genesis 29:6, 'Is he *well*?' according to the Hebrew, 'Is there *peace* to him?' See also Genesis 43:27; Exodus 4:18; 1 Samuel 25:6.

Note 14 (page 124)

On the one hand we see philosophy appropriating religious phrases, and on the other religion appropriating philosophic terms and epithets. We feel suspicious of both. Not that we would fling away a word that is true, or fear to adopt one that honestly expresses our meaning, because these may happen to be fashionable in a certain school. We need not inquire on what anvil the sword was hammered with which we fight. We may ask no questions for conscience sake. But this interchange of terms is of questionable benefit. It tends to mingle together the true and the untrue. It sometimes *indicates,* and at other times *produces,* friendship between parties who ought not to be thus agreed (2 Cor. 6:15). There is danger to the truth of God when philosophy tries to patronise religion, or religion to patronise philosophy. It is assumed by those who are called 'thinking men', and still more by their disciples, that any theological system which is to command the respect (not to say the belief) of modern minds, must be, more or less, a compromise – a concession to religious prejudice on the one hand, and a concession to the advanced opinion and higher criticism of the age, the theologian doing his best, with very unmanageable materials, to construct a system which shall not greatly shock old schools nor excite unnecessary contempt among new, softening down or apologising for the angularities of Scripture, endeavouring to keep it abreast of the improvements of the age, evading the trammels of doctrine, and either rejecting prophetic truth or transmuting the prophetic word into mere symbols for the oracular utterance of commonplace truth, or the mysterious record (in disguise) of well-known history.

Note 15 (page 130)

The *impossibility of the supernatural* is the real idea, latent or announced, in much of the philosophy of the time. From this as the secret basis many have started; to this as the inevitable terminus many are moving. Rejection of the Spirit's personal agency, denial of miracles, dislike of inspiration, Darwinian theories of self-elevation or 'natural selection', are the offspring of one father. Hence, also, the worship of human intellect, the contempt for goodness apart from genius, the unconcealed suspicion that great spirituality is incompatible with great talent, and that a life or book intensely religious must be weak and shallow. Yet, while one large section of modern philosophy goes off in this direction, a considerable part diverges in another, cultivating the supernatural, professing to associate itself with the invisible world, and to fill up imperfect knowledge with the superior information of spirits. Thus, on both sides, there is departure from the divine anchorage, the Bible; the one taking from it in order to have no

supernatural world at all; the other adding to it in order to
have a supernatural world of their own. Truly was it
written, 'I will choose their delusions' (Isa. 66:4); and
again, 'God shall send them strong delusion, that they
should believe a lie' (2 Thess. 2:10-11).

> Hear the just law, the judgement of the skies,
> He that hates truth shall be the dupe of lies;
> And he that *will* be cheated, to the last,
> Delusions strong as hell shall bind him fast.

Thus we see, in our day, sometimes the oscillation
between credulity and scepticism (the poor distracted spirit
flying from one extreme to the other in its search for a
basis of faith); and sometimes the amalgamation of the
two. The result of this is that singular fermentation or
effervescence called 'progress,' which is showing itself
everywhere; according to the advocates of which, religion
is in a transition state, and all modern movements mere
experiments or feelers. The intellect of the age, like
Columbus, is supposed to be steering humanity to an
unknown but golden realm. All is unsettled, and must be
so viewed when we judge the chaos of modern opinion!
Hence the flippancies of free-thinking, the insincerities of
an ill-adjusted formalism, the cravings for innovation, the
incoherencies of self-willed religionism, the puerilities of
amateur-worship, rebellion against theological systems,
and the dishonesties of subscription to creeds not believed
by the subscribers save as the means of livelihood or as a
certificate of character.

Note 16 (page 136)

Because of making such statements, we are sometimes pitied as always preferring the shady aspect of things and persons in the world; looking round us with a melancholy smile; unwilling to take the comfort of any good that life presents. The preceding pages, however, will show this much, that we believe that a Christian man ought always to be joyful, cheerful, genial. But must there not be something lacking in his gladness, or at least a shade flung over it, so long as that awful verse remains in Scripture, 'We are of God, and *the whole world lieth in wickedness*' (1 John 5:19). If the way to life be as narrow as ever, and the way to death as broad; if sin be still what it was when God poured his flood over earth; if Satan be still ruler of the darkness of this world; if error and evil hold hundreds of millions in their sway, and truth and righteousness be still upon the losing side; if pain and sickness and sorrow and death still spread themselves round our globe and enter all human homes; if there be such a place as hell, towards which so many are moving, and in which so many already are; can it be wondered that a Christian's eye is sometimes wet, and his heart not seldom sore? Is it so very unaccountable that all the beautiful things of which earth is full, with all the rich affections and sympathies of life, should be unable to stay his tears? Paul was no gloomy man, of moody spirit, though he said, 'I now tell them, *even weeping,* that they are the enemies of the cross of Christ.' Surely, in this unreclaimed world, and amid the broken, bleeding churches of God, we have objects which (unless we are wholly selfish) may sometimes bring a cloud over our sunniest noons.

Other Christian Heritage titles

Puritan authors

The Heavenly Footman – John Bunyan
Intercession of Christ – John Bunyan
Harmless as Doves – Thomas Watson

With introductions by J. I Packer
The Art of Manfishing – Thomas Boston
The Life of God in the Soul of Man – Henry Scougal
The Mortification of Sin – John Owen
The Pleasantness of a Religious Life – Matthew Henry

With introductions by Maurice Roberts
Christ Crucified – Stephen Charnock
The Temptation of Christ – Thomas Manton
The Life of Faith – Thomas Manton

Edited by Ligon Duncan III
Method For Prayer – Matthew Henry

Other authors
Follow the Lamb – Horatius Bonar
Night of Weeping – Horatius Bonar
Searcher of Hearts – John Newton
According to Promise – C. H. Spurgeon